After Jesus and Paul, Augustine c  figure in the history of Christianity.

Anselm, Aquinas, Petrarch (never without a pocket copy of the Confessions), Luther, Bellarmine, Pascal, and Kierkegaard all stand in the shade of [Augustine's] broad oak. His writings were among the favourite books of Wittgenstein. He was the bête noire of Nietzsche. His psychological analysis anticipated parts of Freud: he first discovered the existence of the sub-conscious.

Henry Chadwick

Augustine entered both the Church and the world as a revolutionary force, and not merely created an epoch in the history of the Church, but... determined the course of its history in the West up to the present day. He had a literary talent... second to none in the annals of the Church. The whole development of Western life, in all its phases, was powerfully affected by his teaching.

B. B. Warfield

Augustine was... a philosopher, theologian, mystic, and poet in one... His lofty powers complemented each other and made the man fascinating in a way difficult to resist. He is a philosopher, but not a cold thinker; he is a theologian, but also a master of the spiritual life; he is a mystic, but also a pastor; he is a poet, but also a controversialist. Every reader thus finds something attractive and even overwhelming: depth of metaphysical intuition, rich abundance of theological proofs, synthetic power and energy, psychological depth shown in spiritual ascents, and a wealth of imagination, sensibility, and mystical fervor.

Agostino Trapè

This is a lively portrait of Augustine's life, work and teachings by a gifted writer who combines deep admiration for the greatest of the early church fathers with an independence of judgement unafraid to criticize his errors. In this impressively comprehensive introduction Augustine retains his fascination. The narrative is enlivened by local colour and by insights from the African bishop's vast corpus of writings often not glimpsed by academic studies. It deserves to whet many a Christian's appetite to grapple with the **Confessions**, **The City of God** and other works at first hand.

David F. Wright
Professor of Patristic and Reformed Christianity
University of Edinburgh

THE APOSTLE FROM AFRICA

The Life and Thought of Augustine of Hippo

David Bentley-Taylor

Christian Focus

Copyright © David Bentley-Taylor 2002

ISBN 1 85792 471 1

Published in 2002 by
Christian Focus Publications, Geanies House,
Fearn, Ross-shire, IV20 1TW, Scotland

www.christianfocus.com

Cover design by Alister MacInnes

Printed and bound by
Cox & Wyman, Reading, Berkshire

All rights reserved. No part of this publication may be reproduced, stored in a retrieval system, or transmitted, in any form, by any means, electronic, mechanical, photocopying, recording or otherwise without the prior permission of the publisher or a license permitting restricted copying. In the U.K. such licenses are issued by the Copyright Licensing Agency, 90 Tottenham Court Road, London WIP 9HE

Contents

Preface 7

1 The Teenager 9

2 The Tormented Professor 17

3 The Great Transformation 31

4 Captured and Called 41

5 Confronting Society and Donatists 53

6 The Preaching Magistrate 61

7 The Truth is God Himself 69

8 Baptism, Communion and the Sabbath 79

9 The Bible Never Lies 85

10 The Moral Battle 91

11 Jerome: Scholar and Linguist 97

12 Petilian: The Persecuted Believer 103

13 A Time to Refrain from Embracing 109

14 Love and Do What You Like 117

15 Pelagius: Champion of Free Will 125

16 Free Will and God's Will 135

17 The City of God 143

18 Monks and Miracles 151

19 Augustine Lives For Ever 157

Maps and Diagrams

Fig. 1 Street Plan of Central Hippo 168

Fig. 2 Numidia in Augustine's time 169

Fig. 3 The Western Mediterranean......................170

Fig. 4 Plan of Augustine's Church in Hippo 171

Preface

Born 700 years after Plato in Athens, and dying 400 years after Jesus' crucifixion in Jerusalem, Augustine belonged to Africa. Just as Plato was outstanding among pre-Christian philosophers, so was Augustine among Christian thinkers, his mind rich as a tropical forest. All round the Mediterranean leading men hung upon his words. Yet at times his errors were deplorable, even horrifying, so that his enemies often had right on their side. Though he strongly promoted the Catholic Church, his evangelical exposition of the faith was so gripping that it inspired Luther, Calvin, and other reformers a thousand years later. So the dramatic story of his life embraces triumph along with tragedy. His insights, predominantly biblical and timeless, are badly needed in our bewildered age, in its turn disposed to neglect truth, despise virtue, and grant impunity to vice.

Around 1980 I completed two manuscripts after many years of research. The first was a biography, *Augustine Wayward Genius*, published by Hodder and Stoughton in England, by Baker Book House in the USA, and by the Word of Life Press in Korea. The second, published only in Korean translation, investigated his basic beliefs. In this new book, I have revised them, shortened them, and fused them into a concise study of both his biography and his convictions.

1

The Teenager

The town of Souk Ahras in eastern Algeria, sixty miles inland from the Mediterranean, marks the site of the ancient city of Tagaste where Augustine was born. From its position, facing south on a steep hillside 2,000 feet above sea level, it commanded a panorama of wooded hills crowned by jagged pinnacles of rock. Below the city the land fell steeply to the gorge of the Medjerda River, rearing up dramatically beyond it till higher ridges closed the view. Within this wide amphitheatre, bisected by the river, were many minor hills cut by ravines, clothed with forests, beautified with cornfields. In winter a cowl of snow rested briefly on the mountains.

Nowadays the North African coast is divided between Morocco, Algeria, Tunisia and Libya, but in Augustine's time the entire region lay within the Roman Empire. Eastern Algeria and western Tunisia formed the province of Numidia. The rest of Tunisia was united with Libya in the original Roman province of Africa with its capital at Carthage, now a suburb of Tunis. The annexation of these regions by the European power had taken place step by step after the destruction of Carthage at the conclusion of the Punic Wars in 146 B.C. Thousands of Romans settled in the conquered lands, augmented by colonies established by Julius Caesar and the Emperor Augustus shortly before the time of Christ. War continued with the Berber tribes of the rugged interior until the frontier of the Empire had been pushed south to the edge of the desert. Settlers intermarried with the original inhabitants and a large population of Romanised Berbers came into existence. Roman financiers bought up extensive tracts of country and the Emperors themselves became the greatest landowners of all. Impressive public buildings were erected, for the Romans held North Africa much longer than they held Britain and to this day it is littered with the remains of their cities, theatres, temples, churches, baths, hippodromes, amphitheatres and aqueducts. Innumerable Roman pillars still reach for the sky.

When North Africa had been part of the Roman Empire for half a millennium, a Tagaste girl named Monica married Patricius, an undistinguished youth, generous at times but hot-tempered and not faithful to his wife. Her family were Catholic Christians, but Patricius was a pagan. Yet she got on well with him and the couple were considered remarkable because they did not quarrel. Monica's friends were often so badly bullied by their husbands that their faces were scarred and bruised. They could not understand how she avoided being battered in the same way. She explained that from the time of her marriage she had regarded Patricius as her master, so she never got angry or resisted him in any way; if his behaviour had been particularly unreasonable, she would wait till he was in a calm mood and then explain herself.

Tagaste lay in the beautiful province of Numidia, mountainous and primitive, dividing the Mediterranean from the Sahara. It was no great advantage to have been born in such a remote place. As one of the settler population, a wide gulf separated Augustine from the indigenous people, apart from those whose families had long absorbed Roman language and culture. The majority of the inhabitants spoke some Berber dialect of the hinterland or else Punic, which had for centuries prevailed in coastal regions ever since the Phoenicians founded

Carthage.

When Augustine started at the local school he had to be forced to work, for he much preferred ball games and for this the masters beat him. His first prayers were that he might not be beaten at school but he so revelled in play that he could not escape the cane. His mother tongue was Latin and gradually he began to enjoy Latin literature, but he loathed the drudgery of learning Greek and never became proficient in it. These studies, however, opened his eyes to evils which soon affected his character and by the time he emerged from childhood he had learned sexual indulgence. Excited by what he saw in the theatre and tempted by the immoralities of the deities he read about at school, his deterioration was rapid. Yet Monica's influence was not altogether eclipsed. 'In my small thoughts upon small matters I had come to delight in the truth, I hated to be wrong, had a vigorous memory, was well trained in speech, delighted in friendship, shunned pain, meanness and ignorance.' Before he reached adolescence the tug-of-war between vice and discipline had started in his heart.

When his primary education had been completed, his parents sensed his intellectual ability and decided to give him the chance of studying in Carthage. The old Phoenician city had experienced a remarkable resurrection to become one of the largest in the Empire. To send their son to study in the capital of Roman Africa was an expense his family could ill afford and their friends much admired them for pursuing the idea. Monica was keen on it because she was anxious about his moral welfare and felt sure that study would help him to become a true Christian.

In order to get together sufficient money they were compelled to take him out of the local school when he was sixteen, so for a year he lived idly at home. This proved a disaster; intellectually he stood still, morally he ran wild. Always a sociable creature, his strong personality tended to make him the central figure in a group of close friends, but he was not yet able to choose friends wisely. With time on his hands and no clear convictions to restrain him, he plunged into rudderless self-indulgence. 'Love and lust boiled within me and swept my youthful immaturity over the precipice of evil desire, to leave me half-drowned in a whirlpool of abominable sins.' Patricius, influenced at last by his wife, was under instruction in the Christian Church but still only superficially moved by its message. One day he saw Augustine stripped at the public baths and went home in delighted excitement to tell Monica he thought they would soon be grandparents. But she did not want him to marry so young in case it interfered with his studies. Too late she urged him not to sin with women, for it was precisely what he had every intention of doing. Unable to distinguish 'the white light of love from the fog of lust', he let himself go. 'I burned for all the satisfactions of hell and sank to the animal in a succession of dark lusts.' Promiscuity left him wretched and restless, arrogant and depressed. His friends were no help. Ashamed to hear others boasting of exploits viler than his own, he set out to imitate them. In such company as he kept, chastity was contemptible, innocence cowardly, evil was pursued just because it was evil, and Monica was powerless to do anything about it. 'The madness of lust took complete control of me.'

When the money was ready, Augustine left Numidia for Carthage. Patricius died shortly afterwards, but he recorded the fact without emotion. However, the loss of his father posed a serious financial threat to his plans, but this was averted by the intervention of Romanianus, a wealthy citizen of Tagaste who had known him from childhood. Long afterwards Augustine revealed the full extent of his help. 'When I was a poor boy, pursuing studies that were not available in our town, you provided me with a home, with funds, and with something better – courage. When I was bereaved of a father, you consoled me with your friendship, roused me with your encouragement, and aided me with your resources. By your favour and friendship you made me almost as renowned and prominent a personage as yourself in our town.'

But once out of Monica's sight he was totally free to continue the vicious way of life on which he had embarked. 'A cauldron of illicit loves leaped and boiled about me.' He deliberately offered his vile deeds to devils and once committed an undefined act of sacrilege in a church. 'What wonder that I became infected with a foul disease?' His passion for the stage only added fuel to his flame. He preferred plays which radically stirred his emotions, 'yet, as if they had been fingernails, their scratching was followed by swelling and inflammation and sores with pus flowing'. In spite of this, his innate ability soon made him a leader in the school of rhetoric. And he became deeply attached to Carthage, its crowded streets, its huge public baths, its wealthy homes with their beautiful mosaic floors, its colossal amphitheatre where helpless men were pitted against professional gladiators and wild beasts, and its theatre seating twenty thousand people.

The curriculum required him to study a book on philosophy by Cicero. 'The one thing that delighted me in Cicero's exhortation was that I should love, seek and embrace not this or that philosophical school but Wisdom itself, whatever it might be. The book excited and inflamed me. In my ardour the only thing I found lacking was that the name of Christ was not there. For with my mother's milk my infant heart had drunk in, and still held deep down in it, that name – and whatever lacked that name, no matter how learned and excellently written and true, could not win me wholly.' This experience drove him to study the Bible for the first time. He had no idea what books it contained but when he began to read them he was repelled by their simplicity. 'They seemed to me unworthy to be compared with the majesty of Cicero.' So he soon gave up.

As a result he had no anchorage for his mind when at the age of eighteen he came across the Manichees, a religious group originating in the previous century in Persia, which combined philosophical speculation and primitive superstition with ideas derived from Judaism and Christianity. 'They declared they would lay aside all authority and by pure and simple reason would bring to God those who were willing to listen to them. What else compelled me to spurn the religion implanted in me as a boy by my parents and to follow these men but that they said we were overawed by superstition and were told to believe rather than to reason, whereas they pressed no one to believe until the truth had been discussed and elucidated? Who would not be enticed by these promises, especially if he were an adolescent with a mind eager for truth but made proud and garrulous by the disputes of learned men at school? Such they found me then, scorning what I took to be old wives' fables and desirous of holding the open and sincere truth which they promised.'

Since Manicheism taught that from the beginning there had been two eternal Principles opposed to one another, God and Satan, it had a ready answer to the problem of evil, feeling no necessity to reconcile its existence with the character of God. Upon this fundamental dualism was grafted a fantastic mythology in which the sun and the moon played their part in the liberation of elements of the kingdom of light imprisoned in the kingdom of darkness. Manicheism was implacably opposed to the Old Testament's representation of God and equally convinced that the text of the New Testament had been corrupted on every page, so it saw no need to defend the Bible against its critics.

From its more devoted adherents it demanded an ascetic way of life, including celibacy, but all its disciplines were inextricably entangled in a jungle of myths. Before long Augustine came to believe in a weird assortment of fantasies: in the Five Elements striving with the Five Dens of Darkness; in God as a kind of material resplendence; and in the ability of Manichean saints to digest figs and then, with groaning and prayer, breathe them out as particles of the Godhead. In later life his verdict was 'I let myself be taken in by fools' and he bitterly regretted that for the next nine years 'I lay tossing in the mud of that deep pit'.

At this point Monica moved back into his life. Now a widow without younger children to care for, she came to Carthage, so dismayed at his adoption of Manichean beliefs that at first she refused to eat with him. She was no match for him in argument but that did not stop her praying, dreaming dreams and enlisting the aid of better-educated people. As she prayed she wept, pressing her face right down on to the ground. In one of her dreams a radiant youth assured her that one day her son would join her, but Augustine was not impressed when she told him about it. He interpreted the dream to mean that she would join him, but she would have none of it. 'No, for it was not said to me "Where he is, you are", but "Where you are, he is"', and he never quite forgot that. Fortunately, this dream encouraged her to have meals with him again. Then she asked a bishop she knew to talk with the boy and set him on the right path. To her regret he refused, feeling it was useless while Augustine was so enamoured with his new ideas. 'Let him alone', he said, 'only pray to the Lord for him. He will himself discover by reading what his error is.' Then the bishop revealed that he had been brought up as a Manichee but eventually found his own way out of the sect. This only made Monica more sure he was the man to help her. To his dismay she burst into tears and he rather lost patience. 'It is impossible that the son of these tears should perish', he said. She could not persuade him, but she took his words as God's answer to her.

For the moment the outlook was unpromising. Proud of his attainments, already a teacher of rhetoric applauded for his poetry, obsessed with the theatre, eager to make money, carrying food to the Manichean elect so that 'in the factory of their stomachs they should turn it into angels and deities', and given over to untempered lusts, he was a constant distress to her. Then all of a sudden his sexual promiscuity ceased. 'In those years I took one woman, not joined to me in lawful marriage, but one whom wandering lust and no particular judgment brought my way. Yet I had but that one woman and I was faithful to her. And with her I learnt by my own experience what a gulf there is between the restraint of the marriage covenant entered into for the sake of children and the mere bargain of a lustful love, where if children come they come unwanted – though when they are born they compel our love.' For a child did come, a boy, whom they called Adeodatus. Augustine never even mentioned the woman's name. She was his sin, not his wife. But he no longer ran wild.

2

The Tormented Professor

From his nineteenth to his twenty-ninth year Augustine remained in such a state of confusion and perversity that he could only look back upon this period with shame. Meanwhile the western half of the Roman Empire, in which he was living, passed into a similarly unhealthy condition. The capable Emperor Valentinian I died when Augustine was twenty-one and for the rest of his life the mantle of imperial responsibility fell upon a succession of infants and boys, guided by their widowed mothers, growing into mediocre young men pathetically lacking the ability to weather the storms which history unleashed upon them.

Augustine's mental agility soon enabled him to outstrip his student contemporaries at Carthage. When a professor of rhetoric warmly commended the *Categories* – Aristotle's introductory treatise on logic – he got hold of a copy and easily mastered it, whereas the others could barely make head or tail of it, even with the aid of teachers drawing diagrams in the dust to illustrate their lectures. His sharp mind gravitated to other sharp minds, so he admired Vindicianus, physician to the late Emperor. It happened that Augustine had just entered a poetic contest and a magician had guaranteed him victory if he made use of his rites and sacrifices. He indignantly refused, won the prize without such aids, and was crowned with a wreath by Vindicianus himself. Attracted by the vitality of the old man's talk, Augustine spoke to him approvingly of horoscope-casters and their books which traced the cause of human triumphs and disasters to the movements of the planets. 'With much fatherly kindness he advised me to throw them away and not waste upon such nonsense time and trouble which could be put to better use.' The occasional success of stargazers in foretelling the future Vindicianus attributed to chance, for which he felt allowance should always be made. Though partially convinced, this conversation did not deflect Augustine from astrological study, even when the doctor's advice was reinforced by the good-natured ridicule of Nebridius, a youth from an estate near Carthage who became one of his closest friends throughout these years. Augustine admired Nebridius for his moral restraint, though he could not imitate it, but at least he had begun to choose his friends more wisely than before.

After graduating from Carthage he became a schoolmaster back home in Tagaste. One of his pupils was a boy named Alypius, a relative of his patron Romanianus. 'He was much attached to me because he thought me kindly and learned, and I to him because of the great bent towards virtue that was marked in him so young.' Alypius' life was destined to be intertwined with his own, but for the moment he was more closely associated with a boy whom he had drawn into Manicheism. When this youth became seriously ill, Augustine would not leave his bedside. As he lay unconscious and apparently at the point of death, his family had him baptized, but his fever abated and as soon as they could talk Augustine poured scorn on what had been done to him. However, the invalid roused himself and in an unexpected outburst of independence told Augustine to stop such talk. It seemed all right to leave, so Augustine withdrew, but shortly afterwards the boy relapsed and died. To this Augustine reacted with extraordinary intensity. 'I raged and wept and was in torment, unable to rest, unable to think.' He became so unhappy that he decided to return to Carthage. Saying nothing to Monica, he talked first to Romanianus. His patron was reluctant for Tagaste to lose him, but finding that he was 'unable to subdue the yearning of a young man striving for what seemed to be better things', he financed the trip.

Back in Carthage Augustine was gradually healed by the passage of time and the company of friends of the type he now preferred. 'All kinds of things rejoiced my soul in their company – to talk and laugh and do each other kindnesses; read pleasant books together; pass from lightest jesting to talk of the deepest things and back again; differ without rancour, as a man might differ with himself, and when most rarely dissension arose find our normal agreement all the sweeter for it; teach each other to learn from each other; be impatient for the return of the absent, and welcome them with joy on their homecoming; these and suchlike things, proceeding from our hearts as we gave affection and received it back, and shown by face, by voice, by the eyes, and a thousand other pleasing ways, kindled a flame which fused our very souls and of many made us one.'

Alypius also moved to Carthage. 'He fell into the way of greeting me when we met and of coming sometimes into my school to listen a while and be off. One day when I was sitting in my usual place with my students in front of me, Alypius came in, greeted me, sat down, and gave his attention to what was being discussed. I had in hand a passage that I was expounding and it suddenly struck me that it could be very well illustrated by a comparison taken from the Games – a comparison which would make the point I was establishing clearer and more amusing, and which involved biting mockery of those who were slaves to that particular insanity.' By 'the Games' he meant the murderous gladiatorial shows at the amphitheatre. He had completely forgotten that Alypius was passionately devoted to these ghastly spectacles, but the latter presumed he had mentioned them for his special benefit. 'Another might have taken it as a reason for being angry with me, but the youth was honest enough to take it as a reason for being angry with himself and for warmer attachment to me.'

He remained for some years in Carthage. Adeodatus and his mother were there too, though he never bothered to mention them. When he was twenty-six he published a series of books entitled *The Beautiful and Fitting*. 'I no longer have them; somehow or other they have been lost.' He dedicated them to a Syrian in Rome of whose great learning in philosophy he had heard. He wished to attain such eminence himself, but his throbbing mind still wandered through a Manichean maze of trivial follies. But he was rather impressed when a Christian named Elpidius came to Carthage debating with the Manichees and produced arguments from the Bible which were not easy to answer. Augustine did not think much of the Manichean retort that the New Testament text had been corrupted by unknown persons. When he himself met Christians he could produce his own awkward ideas. 'Like the argumentative fool that I was, I put to them the question, "Why does the soul err if God created it?"'

He did his best to turn Romanianus into a Manichee but privately confessed to him his own inner turmoil. Romanianus also continued to give him financial support, otherwise he would have been 'held back by kinsfolk whose very life depended on my occupation and by various expenses occasioned by the wretched distress of my relatives'. With this encouragement he read fast and wide in philosophy, mathematics, logic, music and astronomy. He was fascinated by the mysterious constellations and the planets; by solstices, equinoxes and eclipses; by the alternations of night and day; by birds, beasts and fish; by trees and sand. He became increasingly aware that all this could not be harmonized with the fables of Manicheism, and he was grieved by the restless wickedness of men — 'the universe is beautiful about them, but they are vile.' In 383, at the age of twenty-nine, he became professor of rhetoric at Carthage. By then the claim made by Mani, the founder of Manicheism, that the Holy Spirit resided in him personally with plenary authority seemed ridiculous.

At that point there arrived in the city a charming and intelligent man whom Augustine had long desired to meet, Faustus, a bishop of the Manichees. Having with some difficulty arranged to have a thorough discussion with him, Augustine began by setting out the mathematical explanations of astronomical phenomena by which he was attracted, and in no time Faustus realized he was hopelessly outclassed. 'He knew that he did not know these things and he was not ashamed to admit it. He was not entirely ignorant of his own ignorance.' Augustine liked him all the more for his honesty and they saw a lot of each other. The bishop was keenly interested in literature, so the young professor became his teacher and guided his reading. 'But all my effort and determination to make progress in the sect simply fell away through my coming to know this man. Thus Faustus, who had been a snare to many, did without his knowledge or will begin to unbind the snare that held me.'

In his profession he was daily tormented by the rowdiness of the students. 'They break in impudently and like a pack of madmen play havoc with the order which the master has established for the good of his pupils. They commit many outrages, extraordinarily stupid acts, deserving the punishment of the law if custom did not protect them. When I was a student I would not have such habits in myself, but when I became a teacher I had to endure them in others.' Hearing that discipline was better in Rome, which also promised a rise in salary, he decided to leave Africa and work in Italy. He did not even wait to inform Romanianus. His chief problem was how to get away from Monica, who was still living with him. Like her son, she did not do things by halves. She not only went to church on Sunday but twice every day as well, though he had to admit that she lived out her faith in kindly help to others. Furthermore, 'I have no words to express the love she had for me.' So when the time came for him to leave, she simply followed him to the coast and literally clung to him, weeping and refusing to go home. 'She loved to have me with her, as is the way of mothers, but far more than most mothers.' With great difficulty he persuaded her to sleep near the ship, then lied to her and got away in the night. 'The wind blew and filled our sails and the shore dropped from our sight. Next morning she was frantic with grief.' But she did not give up.

His stay in Rome was not a success. As soon as he arrived he fell seriously ill in the home of a hospitable Manichee. 'I very nearly went to hell bearing all the weight of deadly sins which I had committed.' This time he did not ask for baptism, having decided that Christian beliefs were degrading.

Alypius had preceded him to Rome, working as assessor to the Chancellor of the Italian Treasury. Augustine admired him for his high moral principles, especially when he refused to comply with the wishes of a powerful senator in spite of bribes and threats. Manicheism was strong in the city and Augustine stayed on with the sect, though in an unhappy frame of mind. 'When I got settled in Italy I deliberated long as to how truth was to be found: an inextricable thicket confronted me.' He continued to conceive of God in physical terms. He also thought evil possessed its own formless bulk. He could not accept the virgin birth of Christ, because he considered that would have defiled Him. Yet his enthusiasm for Manicheism had evaporated and he even tried to dissuade his kindly host from believing in its fables. He came to feel truth must be beyond human knowledge and that it was best to treat everything as doubtful. He made no contact with Christians in Rome, not even with Jerome, the great biblical scholar, who had arrived there not long before.

To get established as a teacher of rhetoric he took pupils at his home and through them began to be known. But this did not last long. While it was true that Rome was free from the 'riotous incursions of blackguardly youngsters', he discovered there were other defects in student life in the eternal city. They would gang up together and refuse to pay their fees, so a professor could soon find himself in dire straits. 'My heart hated them and not with righteous hatred.' Barely a year after reaching Rome he heard that a job was available up north in Milan, with travel expenses paid. Supported by his Manichean friends, he applied for it and delivered a public oration before the prefect of Rome, an illustrious pagan, who approved of the oration and gave the post to Augustine.

******

'So I came to Milan, to the bishop and devout servant of God, Ambrose, famed among the best men of the whole world.' This was indeed an abrupt change from the company Augustine had kept in Rome. 'That man of God received me as a father and as a bishop welcomed my coming.' Ambrose, his senior by fourteen years, was from a more distinguished family than Augustine. His father had been a Roman official with jurisdiction over wide areas of western Europe. Trained from childhood for leadership in public life, Ambrose soon distinguished himself as a lawyer in Milan. When the Catholic bishop died in 374 he was compelled by popular demand to succeed him. Like many people at the time, he had not been baptized in infancy, so in one week he passed from baptism to the episcopacy and found himself in a position of exceptional influence.

Tragic events had taken place while Augustine was in Rome. The twelve-year-old Emperor Valentinian II and his mother, both living in Milan, ruled Italy and North Africa, but in 383 an army officer in Britain revolted, crossed the Channel and was soon triumphant north of the Alps. There was an obvious danger that he might invade Italy, so the Emperor's mother turned to Ambrose, begging him to go to Trier and persuade the usurper to stay where he was. In this delicate mission Ambrose was remarkably successful, preserving his country from invasion for the time being.

Augustine never explained how he came to meet the bishop beyond saying, 'I was brought by God to him in order that I should be brought by him to God.' But then he traced the course of their friendship in detail. 'I came to love him, not at first as a teacher of truth, but for his kindness towards me.' He had a professional interest in the way Ambrose preached, so he often stood among the crowds of people packed into the church. 'His words I listened to with the greatest care, his matter I held not worthy of attention.' But before long, 'while I was opening my heart to learn how eloquently he spoke, I came to feel, though only gradually, how truly he spoke'. He found it a great help that when preaching from passages in the Old Testament the bishop stressed not so much the literal meaning as the allegorical and spiritual sense to be deduced from it. Perceiving that in this way a reasonable case could be made out for orthodox Christianity, Augustine decided to break his links with Manicheism. Although his mind continued in turmoil, he derived some comfort from the realisation that he had come back to the place where he originally belonged. 'I shall set my foot upon that step on which my parents placed me as a child, until I clearly find the truth.' For the first time in his life he was regularly exposed to intelligent Christian instruction from a man whose character compelled his admiration. 'Nothing of what he said struck me as false, although I did not as yet know whether what he said was true. I held back my heart from accepting anything.'

Then Monica arrived from Africa, braving stormy seas and the long overland journey, still praying, still bemoaning his waywardness, still confident of ultimate triumph. She saw Ambrose for the first time and venerated him like an angel of God for the influence he already had on Augustine. 'When he saw me, he often broke out in her praises, congratulating me that I had such a mother and not realising what sort of a son she had.' Both at home and in Rome she had been accustomed to fast on Saturdays, but this was not the practice in Milan, so Monica wondered what to do. She got Augustine to ask Ambrose about it. 'When I am here,' the bishop replied, 'I do not fast on Saturday, but when I am at Rome, I do.' This completely satisfied her. In Africa she also used to visit the little chapels built in honour of earlier Christian martyrs, going from shrine to shrine with her basket of bread and wine, but she stopped doing so on hearing that Ambrose had forbidden it.

By this time Augustine was eager to have a private talk with the bishop. However, it was not to be. Trained as an administrator rather than a theologian, Ambrose had to keep learning while he taught others, so he combined a certain accessibility with an intensive programme of study. Although visitors were allowed to enter his room, he paid no attention to them but just went ahead with his reading. Several times

Augustine and his friends sat there watching him, but Ambrose remained unaware of the unique opportunity presented to him in the awkward young professor whose mother haunted the church. 'The agitation working in me required that he should be fully at leisure if I were to pour it out before him, and I never found him so.' But he heard him every Sunday in church and gradually it dawned upon him that when mankind was said to have been made in the image of God this did not imply that God had the shape of a human body.

Tormented by the uncertainty, reluctant to commit himself to any beliefs after his disillusionment with the Manichean fables, not at all attracted by Ambrose's celibacy, yet slowly acquiring some sense of the authority of the Bible, he met with constant disappointments in his search for fame and financial security. 'I was in utter misery.' One day when he was writhing with shame over a flattering speech he had to make in praise of the boy Emperor, he spotted a drunken beggar in the street and envied him his scrap of happiness. He said as much to Alypius and Nebridius, his inseparable friends, who had come on to Milan to be with him. The trio were in equal distress, searching desperately for some solution to their need for understanding and moral power.

Each morning he was teaching. Afternoons and evenings were devoted to preparing his lectures and calling on important people whose help he needed. At times he dreamed that his influential friends might get him a governorship so that he could end his financial worries by marrying an heiress. Adeodatus' mother had accompanied him to Milan but no one regarded him as a married man. Alypius was strongly against him being properly married as he felt they would not then be able to go on living together in the pursuit of wisdom. Monica took the opposite view, hoping that after a respectable marriage he might be baptized. Eventually he did propose to a girl and gained her family's consent. As she was still a minor, he agreed to wait two years. At the same time he exerted such an influence upon his men friends that a group of them seriously considered pooling their financial resources and living together in a philosophers' commune. No one was more enthusiastic about this than Romanianus, who had come over from Tagaste to the imperial court on business. His great wealth made the scheme attractive to the others but since some of them were married the whole plan eventually fell through. Then 'she with whom I had lived so long was torn from my side as a hindrance to my forthcoming marriage: she went back to Africa, swearing she would never know another man'. Both of them were heartbroken, for in its way the alliance had not been unsuccessful. Adeodatus, a teenager by this time, remained with his father. However, the two-year wait proved intolerable to Augustine: in bitter grief he took another mistress, but without diminishing his misery. 'Because my will was perverse, it changed to lust, and lust yielded to became habit, and habit not resisted became necessity.'

Enough of his Christian inheritance remained in his mind for him to be sure death was not the end of everything, but he feared he might die before he found the truth. Along with Alypius and Nebridius he was particularly depressed by their vain search for an alternative to the Manichean explanation of the existence of evil. Instead of attributing it to the very nature of things, to an eternally existing force, he began to weigh the suggestion that it is our own free will which causes us to do evil. But then he was dismayed by an answering train of thought. 'Who made me? Was it not my God, who is not only good but goodness itself? What root reason is there for my willing evil and failing to will good, since I was wholly made by my most loving God? If the devil is the author, where does the devil come from? If by his own perverse will he was turned from a good angel into a devil, what was the origin in him of that perverse will, since by the all-good Creator he was made wholly angel?'

He faced the fact that his sinful youth was over and he was now a mature man, 'though so poor a man'. But then his inveterate tendency to think of both God and evil as substances was challenged when he came across the books of Plotinus, the Neo-Platonist philosopher, translated from Greek into Latin by Victorinus, formerly professor of rhetoric at Rome. As he studied them, the tumult raging in his mind was somewhat calmed. He began to reason that evil does not really exist at all. 'There are some things which we call evil because they do not harmonize with other things. Yet these same things do harmonize with still others. In themselves they are good. There is no sanity in those whom anything in creation displeases.' On this basis he tried to settle into the conviction that evil had no independent existence and was merely 'a swerving of the will'. But in his unstable condition the insight was fleeting. Helped to a limited extent by Plotinus, he at last turned to the Epistles of Paul. 'In that pure eloquence I saw One Face and I learned to rejoice with trembling.' Previously he had thought of Christ as a man of marvellous wisdom, but now he was profoundly impressed with the difference between the Platonists and the Scriptures. 'It is one thing to see the land of peace from a wooded mountain-top, yet not find the way to it and struggle hopelessly far from the way with hosts of those fugitive deserters from God, under their leader the Lion and the Dragon, besetting us about and ever lying in wait, and quite another to hold to the way that leads there, a way guarded by the care of our heavenly General.'

He badly needed to talk to someone who had time to listen

and skill to counsel him. Ambrose was obviously too busy but it occurred to him to try Simplicianus, an older man of wide experience whose special talent it was to help those more gifted than himself. 'I told him all the wanderings of my error.' Simplicianus heard him through patiently, but when Augustine mentioned Victorinus' translations the old man interrupted him with the story of how this famous pagan scholar had boldly confessed Christ as his master before he died. Augustine longed to imitate him, but he could not. 'The enemy held my will.' So the interview seemed to have been in vain. The three friends went on living together, Monica keeping house for them. Alypius completed his third term as assessor to the Chancellor and planned in future to sell his legal advice to private clients, just as Augustine sold skill in speaking. They had persuaded Nebridius to join the staff of Verecundus, a schoolmaster in Milan, 'a great friend of us all'. Then one day in August 386, when it chanced that Nebridius was out, a visitor called at the house.

3

The Great Transformation

The visitor was Ponticianus, a man from Africa who held an important position at the imperial court in Milan. As they sat talking he chanced to pick up the copy of Paul's Epistles which Augustine had been reading. He was both surprised and pleased to find such a book lying on the table, and he went on to talk about the Egyptian hermit Anthony, of whom neither Augustine nor Alypius had ever heard. Amazed at their ignorance, he launched into a fuller description of monastic communities not only in the deserts of Egypt but close to Milan itself. As the two men gazed at him in silence he went on to tell the story of two state officials who came across a biography of Anthony and were so impressed that they immediately abandoned their jobs in order to serve God alone. Their fiancées also gave up the idea of marriage, dedicating themselves to God instead.

Ponticianus left without appreciating the effect his words had had upon Augustine. 'I stood naked in my own sight.' Comparing his own long hesitation with the quick response of the men whose story he had just heard, he perceived how twisted and unclean he was, how deeply infected with the disease of lust. Such a dreadful sense of shame and sorrow filled his heart that he had to get away from Alypius. He went out into the garden, but Alypius was so alarmed that he followed him. 'There I was, going mad on my way to sanity.' Tortured by the thought of his mistresses, he again moved away from Alypius and threw himself down weeping under a fig tree at the bottom of the garden. As he lay there in intense distress he heard what seemed to be a child's voice from one of the other houses, saying 'Take and read' over and over again. He rose and went back to where Alypius was sitting, for he had left the copy of Paul's Epistles there. 'I snatched it up, opened it, and in silence read the passage on which my eyes first fell.' It was Romans 13:13-14, 'Not in orgies and drunkenness, not in sexual immorality and debauchery, not in dissension and jealousy. Rather, clothe yourselves with the Lord Jesus Christ and do not think about how to gratify the desires of the sinful nature.' There was no need for him to read on. 'In that instant, with the very ending of the sentence, it was as though a light of utter confidence shone in my heart and all the darkness of uncertainty vanished.' Closing the book, he told Alypius what had happened. Alypius asked to see the verse and read the next one, Romans 14:1, 'Accept him whose faith is weak', which he applied to himself, sharing in his own way in his friend's experience. There and then the proud, immoral Augustine, unhappy and full of doubts, was gone. A new Augustine was born 'in that instant'.

The first act of his Christian life could hardly have been bettered. 'We went in to my mother and told her, to her great joy. We related how it had come about. She was filled with triumphant exultation.' The impossible miracle had actually happened: the professor had found his Master. 'I bowed my neck to Your easy yoke and my shoulders to Your light burden, Christ Jesus, my helper and redeemer. I talked with You as friends talk, my glory, my riches, my salvation, my Lord God.' A conversion had taken place which many have ranked second to that of the Apostle Paul in its significance for the influence of Christianity in the history of mankind.

His immediate concern was to resign from the teaching profession, but he decided it would not be right to do so before the long vacation, due to start in three weeks. Then he was only too relieved to stop lecturing, as he had begun to suffer from chest pains and difficulty in breathing. As soon as term ended he went off to a country house at Cassiciacum lent to him by Verecundus, the schoolmaster with whom Nebridius worked. Seven other men shared this extended holiday from the autumn of 386 to the spring of 387: his brother Navigius and Alypius; his pupils, Trygetius and Licentius, known as 'the boys'; Lastidianus and Rusticus, 'relatives of mine whom I did not wish to be absent, though they are not trained even in grammar, since I believed their common sense was needed'; and Adeodatus, 'the youngest of all, who promises great success, unless my love deceives me'. All of them were from Africa. Licentius, the son of Romanianus, was passionately devoted to poetry and quite capable of leaving in the middle of a meal to compose verses. 'My mother was also with us, a woman in sex, with the faith of a man, the serenity of great age, the love of a mother, the piety of a Christian.' She played a full part in some of their discussions, which were held in the bathhouse when the weather was inclement. 'Very well expressed', he commented with a smile after one of her remarks, 'No better answer to my question could have been expected.' Once when she joined the group late and asked how their debate was going, he insisted in spite of her protests that her presence and her question should be recorded by the secretaries who were always with them. At other times she had to stop the talk and push the men in to meals.

They were well served by farm hands, kitchen helpers, and a boy who used to run and call them when food was ready. Weather permitting, they strolled in the fields or sat under the shade of a tree. When their discussions went on after sunset, lamps were brought out to make sure the secretaries missed nothing.

But there was plenty of fun and laughter as well as serious talk.

During this breathing space at Cassiciacum, Augustine began to write books, though he was such a novice in Christian matters that they were more philosophical than biblical. Indeed Alypius at first maintained that the quality of his writing would be impaired if he so much as mentioned Jesus Christ. Augustine's mind needed time to catch up with his heart. Having for so long been what he called 'a blind, raging snarler against the Scriptures', he was not accustomed to uttering Christian statements, but he learnt rapidly as he meditated with delight on the Psalms. Then this was rudely interrupted by an attack of toothache which became so agonising that he could not even speak. He wrote down an urgent appeal to the others to pray for him and 'as soon as we had gone on our knees in all simplicity, the pain went'.

On his thirty-second birthday, 'after a breakfast light enough not to impede our powers of thinking', he called them together for discussions which continued for three days and were incorporated in *The Happy Life*, the first of all the books he wrote as a Christian to be completed. At one point he threw out the question, 'Who really possesses God?' Little Trygetius, never at a loss for words, blurted out, 'He who does what God wills to be done', and the rustic relatives agreed. Licentius preferred, 'He who lives an upright life', while Adeodatus suggested, 'He who has a spirit free from uncleanness.' Monica approved all these opinions, especially the last one. Adeodatus explained that he meant 'one who lives chastely' and, when this too was challenged, added 'How can someone be chaste who refrains only from illicit intercourse but does not desist from a steady pollution of the soul from other sins?' He insisted that 'He is truly chaste who keeps God in mind and devotes himself to Him alone'. Augustine made sure the secretaries got that down.

During the winter months at Cassiciacum he often lay thinking late into the night or in the pre-dawn hours. On one of these occasions he was listening to water as it ran through wooden channels behind the bathhouse, when Licentius made a movement which showed that he was awake and also disturbed some mice. Trygetius proved to be awake as well, so they talked till dawn began to steal in through the windows, discussing 'how it is that, though God has a care for human affairs, perversity is so serious'. It bothered them that fleas are marvellously made, yet human life is in such disorder. Excited by what Augustine was saying, Licentius leapt out of bed and stood over Trygetius demanding, 'I am asking you now, "Is God just?"' Trygetius was too sleepy or too surprised to answer, so Licentius lay down again complaining that the matter had not been satisfactorily explained.

When daylight came the boys got up and Augustine 'shedding tears, spent some time in prayer', but he was disturbed by Licentius singing Psalm 80:7 with gusto – 'Restore us, O God Almighty; make Your face shine upon us, that we may be saved.' The previous evening Monica had reproved him for singing it over and over again in the toilet. 'He chanted it a little more loudly than our mother could bear such words to be repeatedly chanted in that place.'

They had their daily time of prayer together and were moving to the bathhouse to continue discussion when they stopped to watch two cocks fighting in front of the door. This provoked the question, 'Why do all cocks behave in this way?' Augustine took the rest of the day quietly on account of chest pains, though as usual he managed to work through half a book of Virgil with the boys before the evening meal.

Soliloquies, the last of the books he wrote at Cassiciacum, 'in which I question and answer myself about those truths I was specially eager to know, as if there were two of us – Reason and I – whereas I was by myself', began with a prayer which epitomized the change that was coming over his outlook. 'Hear, O hear me, my God, my Lord, my King. Hear me my Father, my Hope, my Salvation, my Light, my Life, hear, O hear me.' God and the Bible had begun to compete with Virgil, Cicero and the philosophers for the control of his mind during that carefree withdrawal from responsibilities and duties in society which he fondly anticipated would be normal for his new way of life.

In preparation for his forthcoming baptism, Augustine wrote to Ambrose asking which part of the Bible he ought to be studying. 'He told me to read Isaiah the prophet, I imagine because he more clearly foretells the calling of the Gentiles than the other Old Testament writers; but I did not understand the first part of his book and, thinking it would be all of the same kind, put it aside, meaning to return to it when I should be more practised in the Lord's way of speech.' So once again Ambrose, who had greatly helped Augustine by his preaching, proved unable to give him the personal counsel he needed. Temperamentally they were very different. The great man who had lived such a steady Christian life from his youth was not quite at his best in dealing with a professor whose background was so different. This did not deter him from baptising Augustine and Alypius by threefold immersion in the name of the Father, the Son and the Holy Spirit at Easter 387. 'We also took with us the boy Adeodatus, carnally begotten by me in sin. He was barely fifteen, yet he was more intelligent than many a grave and learned man. In this I am but acknowledging to You Your own gifts, O Lord my God, Creator of all and powerful to reshape our shapelessness: for I had no part in that boy but the sin. That he had been brought up by us in Your way was because You had inspired us, no other. We took him along with us, the same age as ourselves in Your grace, to be brought up in Your discipline, and we were baptized and all anxiety as to our past fled away.'

******

After his baptism, Augustine, free from teaching rhetoric, continued in Milan the life of study, prayer and discussion which he had established at Cassiciacum. Never again did he refer either to his second mistress or to his child fiancée. He repeatedly tried his hand as an author, not always with success: one book he eventually lost; with another he was not satisfied; of a third he later said, 'It is so obscure that even my own attention flags as I read it.'

Meanwhile the western half of the Roman Empire was again in great danger. The usurper from Britain moved his troops skilfully through the Alps and Italy fell to him without a major battle. During these anxious days, Augustine's company was reinforced by another young man from Tagaste, a civil servant named Evodius, who had given up his job since his conversion and baptism. To some extent Evodius took the place of Nebridius, who had missed the crucial interview with Ponticianus as well as the months at Cassiciacum. 'We kept together, meaning to live together in our devout purpose. We thought deeply as to the place where we might serve God most usefully. As a result we started back for Africa.'

Augustine did not explain in detail the reasons for this momentous decision. Monica naturally wanted to get home and eventually to be buried alongside her husband. And the whole group were united by their African origin as well as their Christian faith. Their roots were not in Europe: indeed all of

The Apostle From Africa

them probably had Berbers among their ancestors. Furthermore, Augustine had had a good chance to observe Ambrose, his heavy duties as minister of a large city church, his many sermons and innumerable visitors, his lack of privacy for study and prayer, and his involvement in secular affairs. This was a far cry from the pattern of life he had so much enjoyed since resigning his professorship and he had no intention of getting similarly entangled in administrative or political matters. He was much more attracted by the ways of the hermit Anthony and the monasteries in the Egyptian desert, news of which had played such a vital part in his conversion.

So they left Milan and travelled down to Rome, a trip of some three hundred miles. Then they moved out to Ostia, the old port at the mouth of the Tiber, ready to embark for Carthage. As before, Monica was the only woman in the party. Of the rest 'she took as much care as if she had been the mother of us all and served us as if she had been the daughter of us all'. Though she was only fifty-six, this was a considerable age for a woman at that time and they thought of her as elderly.

One day 'she and I stood leaning in a window which looked inwards to the garden within the house where we were staying at Ostia; for there we were away from everybody, resting for the sea voyage from the weariness of our long journey by land. There we talked together, she and I alone, in deep joy.' Describing the occasion long afterwards, Augustine recalled that they discussed what the eternal life of Christians would be like in heaven. He did the talking, but Monica shared it all with him and then she said, 'Son, for my own part I no longer find joy in anything in this world. What I am still to do here and why I am here, I know not.' Now that he was a Catholic Christian she felt her life's work was finished.

Barely a week later, while they still waited at Ostia, she

became ill. Soon afterwards she said to Navigius and Augustine, 'Here you will bury your mother.' They were surprised that she did not seem concerned at the prospect of dying so far from Tagaste. 'Nothing is far from God', she said, 'and I have no fear that He will not know at the end of the world from what place He is to raise me up.' As Augustine was looking after her she suddenly remarked what a loving and dutiful son he had been, saying that he had never spoken harshly to her. 'But what possible comparison was there between the honour I showed her and the service she had rendered me?'

On the ninth day of her illness, while they were all standing round her bed, she died. Adeodatus burst into tears but Augustine checked him and thereby restrained his own. Evodius started to chant Psalm 101 and they all joined in. As friends came round to the house Augustine found relief in talking to them while arrangements for the funeral went ahead. At the graveside he did not weep, not even during the final prayers while her body lay by the open grave. When all was over he had a bath and then fell fast asleep. On waking he lay in bed repeating the verses of an evening hymn Ambrose had written. And then at last he did what he had stopped Adeodatus doing. 'I found solace in weeping both about her and for her, about myself and for myself. I no longer tried to check my tears, but let them flow as they would, making them a pillow for my heart, and it rested upon them.' He thought no one would blame him that for a while 'I wept for my mother, now dead and departed from my sight, who had wept so many years for me that I should live for ever in God's sight.'

With Monica's passing the long introductory stage of Augustine's life was over.

4

Captured and Called

Turmoil on the coast of Italy prevented them sailing to Carthage, so for the time being Augustine and his friends returned to Rome, where he continued the habit of writing which he had by this time formed. Having been long hoodwinked by the Manicheans, he wanted to refute their teaching and expose the moral weakness to which he felt it led, for he was impressed by the different standard of behaviour he found among responsible Catholics. On the other hand he was not attracted by what he saw of the life of bishops and priests in Rome. Pestered as they were by such crowds of needy people, he considered it was impossible for them to live a truly holy life or enjoy the kind of inward tranquillity which he had come to value. He had no intention of getting involved in that way himself. What fascinated him were the communities of celibate men, holding everything in common, supporting themselves by manual labour, giving all they could to the poor, and passing their time in prayer, reading, and spiritual conference. He had glimpsed this way of living while he was still in Milan and he now found similar institutions for widows and unmarried girls, who gained their livelihood by spinning and weaving. For the moment he just watched what was going on, taking no prominent part in the work of the Church in Rome and making no lasting friendships there.

During 388, Theodosius, the ruler of the eastern part of the Roman Empire, reconquered Italy and in the course of this further upheaval Augustine and his friends slipped across to Africa. He had been five years away and was so pleased to be back that he never left his homeland again. He found he had not been entirely forgotten in Carthage. He came across a former student of his who had himself become a teacher. He told Augustine that one evening he had been greatly troubled by his inability to understand a passage of Cicero which he was to expound next morning, but in the night he had a dream in which Augustine appeared to him and explained it all.

He stayed for a while in the home of a prominent man named Innocentius, who had recently suffered dreadfully in an operation for fistulas in the rectum. Medical treatment had continued but eventually his doctor confessed that one ulcer was inaccessible without a further operation. The patient was so terrified that a consultant from Alexandria was brought in, but he agreed that a fresh incision must be made. Sympathetic visitors came every evening, including a bishop and a deacon who was soon to become bishop of Carthage. The night before the operation Innocentius was so unnerved that he invited them all to return in the morning to be present at his death. They did their best to reassure him, urging him to trust in the Lord, and then they prayed together. 'When we knelt down in the usual way and bent towards the ground, Innocentius hurled himself forward as if someone had pushed him flat on his face and began to pray. All I could do was to say this brief sentence in my heart, "Lord, what prayers of Your people do You hear, if You do not hear these?" We rose from our knees and after receiving the bishop's blessing we left, the sick man entreating his visitors to come back in the morning. They arrived as they had promised. The surgeons entered. All preparations had been made which that fateful hour demanded. The fearful instruments were produced, while we all sat there in dumbfounded suspense.

While his body was being laid in position, the visitors whose authority was greatest tried to raise the patient's drooping spirits with words of encouragement. The bandages were untied and the place was bared. The surgeon examined it, knife in hand, ready for the incision.' But it was not necessary. Their prayers had been answered. They rejoiced and wept together as they gave thanks to God.

Thus encouraged the group went on to Tagaste and settled down at Augustine's old home to a community life in which all their possessions were shared. Possidius, a youth who joined them at that time and was destined to be Augustine's colleague for the next forty years, remembered that 'he persevered there for nearly three years, living for God in fasting, prayer and good works, meditating day and night on the laws of the Lord, and imparting to others what God revealed to him during contemplation and prayer'. Intensive Bible study took the place of formal theological training, while in leading the group Augustine gained experience as a preacher. Such was the impression he made on others that whenever he appeared to be at leisure people would take the opportunity of asking him about any matter that was perplexing them, such as 'Is God the creator of evil?', 'Is fear a sin?', or 'Why did the Son of God appear as a man and the Holy Spirit as a dove?' From time to time he dictated answers to eighty-three such questions which were eventually collected into a book. These three years began to change him from being an intellectual acquainted with secular literature into a Christian teacher characterized by phenomenal knowledge of the Bible.

But it was at Tagaste in 390 that he suffered his most grievous loss. Every reference in his writings to Adeodatus shows the affection and admiration he had for his son. He produced a booklet in the form of a dialogue between the two of them, which gives a delightful impression of the boy's relationship with his father. When Augustine apologized to him for sharpening their minds by indulging in verbal play after the Socratic manner, Adeodatus replied, 'Go on as you have begun, for I shall never consider unworthy of attention anything you may think it necessary to say or do.' He also managed to correct Augustine on the precise meaning of a Punic word. 'All the ideas which are put into the mouth of the other party to the dialogue were truly his, though he was but sixteen', Augustine explained long after. 'I had experience of many other remarkable qualities in him. His great intelligence filled me with a kind of awe, and who but God could have been the maker of things so wonderful? But You took him early from this earth and I think of him utterly without anxiety, for there is nothing in his boyhood or youth to cause me to fear.' And that is all we shall ever know about the fate of Adeodatus, for Augustine never referred to him again.

Many people in Numidia had an eye on the community of dedicated men at Tagaste. Their leader's dynamic personality, reputation for learning and ability as a writer were widely known. So Augustine took care to avoid going to towns which had no bishop. He had not forgotten the way Ambrose had been forced into a position of responsibility in Church and State. Not being one who enjoyed travelling, he was content to stay where he was unless some very good reason presented itself.

Early in 391, when he was thirty-seven years old, it did seem desirable that he should go to the port of Hippo. Somebody there was anxious to meet him in the belief that if only he could hear the word of God from Augustine he would be able to give up his job and become a full-time Christian. The Church at Hippo already had a highly respected leader in Bishop Valerius, so there were no good grounds for keeping away from it, and in any case Augustine was on the lookout for a more suitable location for his group than remote Tagaste. So he set off on horseback for the sixty-mile journey over the hill behind the city, down through the woods which blanketed the long ridges descending towards the coast, and across the plain to Hippo.

His talks with the man he had come to see were not successful, as the latter kept deferring the decision at which he had hinted. When Sunday came round, Augustine went to church to hear the bishop preach. He was rather more conspicuous than he had expected. Valerius, only too well aware of his presence, seized the opportunity to tell the people there was urgent need for a second ordained man in Hippo. At once the congregation laid hands on Augustine and brought him to the front amid general acclamation. There was no escape: he was caught, just as Ambrose had been, and ordained on the spot. In the emotion of the moment he could not restrain his tears. Some thought this was because he had not been made a bishop right away, but the real reason was that he knew ordination meant the end of his dream of a tranquil Christian life, withdrawn from the pressures and strife of the world.

When it was all over he frankly told Valerius he was a mere beginner in Christian matters whose past life had not prepared him for the kind of role into which he had suddenly been thrust. 'I did not at any earlier period know how great was my unfitness for the arduous work which now disquiets and crushes my spirit. You think me qualified, whilst I know myself better. I unreservedly believe the doctrines pertaining to our salvation, but my difficulty is how to use this truth for the salvation of others.' He begged to be allowed a short time for prayer and preparation. This was granted in spite of the fears of some people that he might yet elude them.

And so it came about that Augustine moved permanently to

Hippo on the Mediterranean, lying between hills at the mouth of the Seybouse River with a 3,000 foot mountain immediately to the north. It was not a town to be compared with Carthage, Rome, or Milan, but it was at least less insignificant than Tagaste, which from that time dropped out of his story. In succeeding ages he was to be remembered as 'Augustine of Hippo'.

Bishop Valerius was a mild man, admired by all who have left any account of him. Well aware of his own limited gifts, he was delighted to have Augustine alongside him. Free from envy, he was only too ready to give full scope to the younger man. In those days Christianity was in the ascendant. From its obscure origins in the Middle East it had grown steadily in Mediterranean lands, surviving a series of imperial persecutions. Then came its most severe test, the fiercer persecution after the year 300, leading to the extraordinary triumph of the Church when the Emperor Constantine professed the faith and Catholic Christianity acquired such strong official support that it gradually became the recognized religion. 'The Roman Empire, by God's gracious favour, became Christian.'

Peace came to the harassed communities. Large churches were erected everywhere. Bishops became prominent members of society. Colossal numbers of people were baptized. 'Almost all the nobility are within the church, along with many wise and learned men, scientists and philosophers.' Yet Augustine admitted that 'throughout the world blameless Christians are mingled with Christians unworthy of the name, crowds of heathen assuming the Christian religion, false Christians and pretended Christians, who by their unprincipled behaviour cause the name of Christian and Catholic to be defamed' (*Letter 53:6, City 20:19*). With surprising frequency he alluded to 'wicked and immoral clergy' and to selfish bishops 'who enjoy the secular advantages of their office' (*Letter 208:2,3*). And he repeatedly quoted Christ's parable about the good seed and the weeds in Matthew 13:24-30, which forbade trying to separate them, saying 'Let both grow together until the harvest'. So his advice was 'You see weeds among the wheat, evil Christians among good Christians? Do you want to root out the evil ones? Be quiet! This is not the harvest time. That time will come. Why vex yourselves? On us God has laid the duty of gathering the flock. To Himself he has reserved the work of final separation' (*Sermon 23:1, Letter 208:6*).

******

At Hippo, Augustine found public opinion had become so tolerant of drunkenness that it was even permitted in church. Shortly before the annual feast day, he preached an aggressive sermon against this relaxation of morals, bluntly stating that drunkenness was sin and drunkenness in church a crime.

The news of what he had said spread through the town and aroused such hostility that a large crowd assembled to listen to him on the day before the feast. Helpers stood close by with Bible manuscripts open at passages he had selected. His graphic account of what followed reveals the seriousness with which he took the task of expounding the word of God and the secret of the immense influence he soon came to wield. In a tense atmosphere he talked for a long time about not turning the house of God into a den of thieves, skilfully analysed the drunken revelry described in Exodus 32 – 'I took the manuscript from the attendant and read that whole passage' – and in a commanding manner enforced upon his hearers numerous Old and New Testament verses, including Paul's statement that drunkards will not inherit the kingdom of God. He then reminded them of Christ's humiliation, His pierced hands and crown of thorns, His cross and His blood. 'In this appeal I put forth all the power in thought and utterance which our Saviour was pleased to supply in so great and hazardous an emergency. Moved by the tears which they began to shed, I myself could not refrain from following their example. And when we had thus wept together, I concluded my sermon with full persuasion that they would be restrained by it from the abuses I had denounced.'

Next day, however, the outlook was less hopeful, for many resented the prohibition of celebrations to which they had become accustomed. 'Then the Lord showed me that He does not leave us alone.' The very men who were most vocal in opposition came to him privately before he had to speak in public and by talking to them in a kindly way he won them over to his viewpoint. Fortified by their support, he abandoned the message he had intended to give. Instead he explained to the people how these revels had originated after persecution ceased earlier in the century and large numbers of pagans entered the Church, who then celebrated Christian festivals in much the same way as they had heathen ones. He urged them to imitate overseas churches in this matter, but at that they appealed to the 'daily excess in the use of wine in the church of the blessed Apostle Peter'. Augustine had to admit how difficult it had proved to suppress the evil at Rome because in such a city there were many carnally-minded people. 'If we want to honour the Apostle Peter, I continued, we ought to hear his words and look more to the epistles by which his mind is made known to us than to the place of worship by which it is not made known', and he skilfully reinforced his argument by reading to them I Peter 4:1-3 with its repudiation of drunken revels. He then called everyone together at noon to celebrate the festival not by self-indulgence but by the reading of the word of God and the singing of psalms.

A very large company assembled. The reading and singing took place before Valerius and Augustine entered the church. 'Then the old man constrained me by his express command to say something to the people, from which I would rather have been excused as I was longing for the close of the anxieties of the day. I delivered a short discourse to express our gratitude to God.'

Before long the inevitable happened: Valerius asked him to preach on Sundays. Once launched upon this task he gathered up all the experience of his darker days and discovered a satisfying outlet for the findings of his Bible study. The result was an avalanche of sermons, taken down by secretaries as they were delivered, about a thousand of which are still extant today.

Valerius was delighted. He was himself a Greek whose knowledge of Latin was so slight that it had proved to be of little use to him. He regarded the coming of Augustine as an act of God in answer to his prayers for the renewal of the Church through sound instruction. It was unknown in Africa for someone else to preach when the bishop was present and he was criticized for allowing it. But he saw the people needed it, so he gave Augustine his full support and encouraged him to hold public discussions in church as well. This policy was dramatically vindicated in August 392. There had been a movement towards Manicheism ever since a man named Fortunatus had begun preaching in Hippo. Augustine was asked to confront him. From previous knowledge of Augustine, Fortunatus was rather anxious at the prospect, but his followers were so enthusiastic that he could hardly refuse. For two days they argued before a large audience. 'I affirmed that the evil of mankind had sprung from the choice of the will. He on the other hand tried to show that the nature of evil is co-eternal with God.' In the end Fortunatus withdrew on the plea of consulting his colleagues, left the city at once, and never returned. Such a triumph spread Augustine's fame throughout North Africa and overseas. It was a difficult time for Catholic Christianity, so to have such a redoubtable champion as Augustine step into the arena was like life from the dead. His books and booklets were eagerly read and copies of his sermons widely distributed. 'So much authority was attributed to me that whenever it was necessary for someone to speak to the people and I was present, I was seldom allowed to be silent and listen to others.' He was also constantly teaching those who lived with him in the monastery which Valerius had encouraged him to establish alongside the church, where he was already training a number of dedicated men whose influence was destined to be far-reaching.

Valerius grew older and his health began to fail. He wrote to the primate of Roman Africa, suggesting that Augustine be made assistant bishop of Hippo. Augustine himself remained hesitant, believing it to be contrary to the custom of the Church to have two bishops in one town, but at length he was induced to consent. And so, by the strong light shining out of Numidia, leading men everywhere became aware that a new star of the first magnitude had risen in the Christian sky. When the African bishops assembled for a general council at Hippo in December 393, Augustine was given the opportunity of addressing them. His talk contained seventy quotations from the Bible.

That same year he had been working on the book of Genesis. At Tagaste he had attempted an allegorical interpretation of it, but then he decided to add an explanation of its literal meaning. 'I wanted to test my capabilities in this most taxing and difficult work, but in explaining the Scriptures my inexperience collapsed under the weight of so heavy a load and before I had finished one volume I rested from this labour which I could not endure.' He switched his attention to the Sermon on the Mount and in 394 produced a commentary on it, devoting an average of half a page to every verse. Then, while in Carthage during the heat of summer, he delivered a series of addresses on the Epistle to the Romans and wrote a book answering the questions people put to him afterwards. Encouraged by this, he added a brief commentary on the Epistle to the Galatians, giving a simple explanation of each verse. Next he turned back to the Epistle to the Romans, planning to expound the whole of it in the same way, but once again found that he did not have the gifts such work demanded. 'Discouraged by the magnitude and labour of the task, I stopped.' Having covered only the first seven verses, he confessed with relief, 'I lapsed into easier things.' He was no doubt right in thinking that his talent was for the pastoral application of Scripture rather than for detailed, scholarly exposition, for which his ignorance of Hebrew and limited knowledge of Greek were severe handicaps. Never again did he find time or inclination to comment systematically on any of Paul's Epistles.

5

Confronting Society and Donatists

In 395 Valerius died and for the next 35 years Augustine found himself sole bishop of Hippo in an Empire sliding into chaos, doomed to collapse before the onslaught of its enemies.

The duties of the bishop of Hippo were different from what the title might imply today. 'My special charge does not extend beyond the Church of Hippo', explained Augustine. 'In other towns I interfere only so far as is permitted or enjoined by my brethren bearing the same priestly office, the bishops of these towns.' In spite of some oversight of the surrounding villages, frequent visits to Carthage and regular attendance at councils of bishops held in various towns, he was primarily the minister of one church, occupied in the pastoral care of its large congregation and in a heavy programme of preaching, teaching and writing.

However, Augustine was a prominent figure in the city as well as in the church. Initially he had obtained the consent of the people to his request that he should be left undisturbed to study the Scriptures for five days every week. After a very short time the agreement became a dead letter. He was so regularly required to settle disputes about money, property or cattle that he often felt weakened in the discharge of his directly Christian responsibilities by 'the darkness and confusion arising from secular occupations'. He envied the monks who had isolated themselves on an island off the coast of Sardinia. 'I can scarcely breathe for the pressure of such duties imposed upon me.' His mornings were mostly spent sitting in court as an arbitrator, a magistrate. Sometimes he would devote an entire day to examining case after case, without even stopping for food. But, however irksome the task may have been, it provided admirable preparation for his preaching by giving him detailed insight into the lives of those he addressed in church.

Year after year he had the opportunity to influence society. 'Crowds of common people possessing no great strength of intellect' lay wide open to the Christian message: entertainers dancing on the tightrope, barbers with hair accumulating round their feet, spectators watching blood spilt in amphitheatres, oarsmen singing boat songs on the river, highwaymen lying in ambush, parents abandoning tiny children, youths apparently possessing characteristics of both sexes, women with breast cancer wondering about surgery, and families hoping to ward off evil influence by hanging up sacred earth from Jerusalem in their bedrooms.

Idolatry was actively discouraged by the authorities, the Empire was visibly disintegrating, and the religion the state had adopted almost a century before offered a port in the world's storm. 'The name of Christ is on the lips of every man: it is invoked by the soldier to nerve himself for battle, by the husband to establish his authority, by the rich man when he gives, by the poor when he receives, by the drunkard at his wine cup, by the beggar at the gate; all frequently use the name of Christ.'

Yet Augustine well knew that most of these people had never discovered the truth of the gospel. 'Many of them place their happiness in song, in the music of lyre and flute. If these are missing, they are wretched. If present, they are so transported with joy that however long the music of a singer lasts, his admirers vie with each other to hear him, crowd each other, and fight for seats to get nearer to him. But they retain nothing lastingly. Sounds only touch them and die away, while those who do not cling to wisdom suffer that punishment which consists in the mind being ruled by passion and robbed of its store of virtue. They despair of finding any truth at all and cling to the darkness of their folly, while the passions rule like tyrants, throwing the whole life into confusion as they are drugged and tortured by fear, desire, greed and self-indulgence. Freedom consists in embracing the truth, submitting to the truth, for it is God Himself who frees us from the state of sin' (*Choice 2:13:35* to *2:14:38* and *1:11:22*).

Problems which have troubled Christians in all ages were constantly brought to Augustine. 'As to killing others to defend one's own life, I do not approve of this unless one is a soldier or public functionary acting not for himself but in defence of others.' He maintained that the precept 'Do not resist an evil person' (Matt. 5:39) was given to prevent us from taking revenge, 'not to make us neglect the duty of restraining men from sin'. And at a time when comprehensive insurance policies were not available he did his best to encourage those who were alarmed at the possibility of being held accountable if tragedies occurred. 'God forbid that we should be blamed for accidents which, without our desire, happen to others through things done by us or found in our possession which are in themselves good and lawful. In that event we ought to have no iron implements for the house or field, lest someone should by them lose his life or take another's; no rope or tree on our premises, lest someone hang himself; no window in our house, lest someone throw himself down from it; the oxen of a Christian should have no horns, his horses no hoofs and his dogs no teeth.'

In all his work in Numidia Augustine suffered from the handicap of speaking only Latin, a language imported five hundred years before when North Africa was annexed to the

Roman Empire. Before 1000 B.C. the native tribes spoke various Berber languages. When the coastal regions were penetrated by the Phoenicians they brought Punic, which grew to be the mother tongue of many Berbers, but not of those in the mountainous interior. Then came Latin, pushing Punic back as Punic had pushed back the native dialects. There was some overlapping, yet this threefold linguistic division of society – Berber, Punic and Latin – has to be borne in mind in evaluating the impact Augustine was able to make upon his contemporaries. The vastness of Numidia and the nature of its terrain ensured that there were limits to the influence of Roman culture, Roman language and the Roman Catholic Church.

******

Ambrose died in 397 and was succeeded as bishop of Milan by old Simplicianus, whom Augustine always remembered with gratitude. He himself was in poor health at the time. 'I am confined to bed. I can neither walk nor stand nor sit because of the pain and swelling of a boil. Pray for me that I may not waste my days through want of self-control and that I may bear my nights with patience.' The loss of Ambrose did not affect him much for they had never become close friends or corresponded since Augustine's return to Africa.

Most of Augustine's correspondents asked respectfully for his advice, like a young man concerned to know whether or not to fast on Saturdays. He told him that he expected all Christians to fast on Easter Saturday but that on other Saturdays only the church at Rome and a few other places fasted, sometimes adding Wednesday and Friday fasts as well. In some monasteries which fasted for five days every week, Saturday and 'the Lord's day' were excluded. Fasting on what we call Sunday he ruled out altogether as a Manichean custom. 'If I be asked what is my own opinion in this matter, I answer, after carefully pondering the question, that in the New Testament I see that fasting is enjoined, but I do not discover any rule definitely laid down by the Lord or the apostles as to days on which we ought, or ought not, to fast.'

Because there was no postal service, writing letters was not a daily task for Augustine. What did confront him daily was the remarkable success of the free church in Numidia, the Donatist Church, so called after its leader when it broke from the Catholic Church eighty years earlier. He regarded Donatists as criminals who had rent the Lord's tunic, which even his executioners refrained from doing. He never recognized believers who were not Catholics as brothers and sisters in Christ, never shared in their gatherings for worship or appreciated the warmth of their home life. To him they were enemies. 'God is our Father and the Church our Mother, by whom we are born to eternal life. Our Mother is the Church and her breasts are the two Testaments of the Divine Scriptures' (*Homily 3:1*). Constant use of such statements had the effect of glorifying the visible church, 'our Catholic Mother' (*Confessions 6:3*). His delight at the triumph of this Universal Church was matched by his distress that in Africa it had been rent in two by 'the great scandal of schism'. To him the outstanding need of the time was the wiping out of this 'tumour'. All he could contemplate was the surrender of the other side, 'that they may have within the peace of the Church that holy sacrament for their salvation which they meanwhile have beyond the pale of the Church for their destruction'. Not for a moment could he consider mutual recognition and respect between Catholics and Donatists, even though he admitted 'they believe just what we believe'. Both Churches were episcopal, administering baptism and celebrating holy communion in the same manner. But the Donatist fellowship was less Roman than the Catholic Church and thus less European, less colonial, less confined to the Latin language. It had more simple, uneducated people, more country people, for its main strength lay back in the mountains.

On one occasion Augustine discussed the question of disunity with a number of Donatist leaders, going over with them the events which had led to the emergence of their Church some forty years before he was born. Not long afterwards he spent a whole day with the same men, reading to them from the civil and ecclesiastical records of the past with the aim of convincing them that the Church in which they had been brought up was no true Church at all. He had what he claimed were the facts at his fingertips and he was a scholar talking to countrymen from the mountains, ignorant of history. Having completed his indictment, he pointed the moral. 'Nothing compels you to remain in such a fatal schism, if you would but subdue the lust of the flesh in order to win the spiritual kingdom and escape from eternal punishment. Go now and take counsel together. Find what you can say in reply.' Of course they could not find anything to say. They just waited till the great man had gone and then continued as before.

The following year Augustine got in touch with Fortunius, the Donatist bishop, suggesting a conference. 'He did not decline the visit. I therefore went to him, because I thought it due to his age that I should go to him instead of insisting upon his first coming to me.' Alypius and others were with him and they all sat down in Fortunius' house, which was then invaded by crowds of onlookers, few of whom came in a genuine spirit of enquiry. 'Everything was thrown into confusion by the noise of men speaking loudly.'

Augustine tried to have the proceedings properly recorded

but heckling was so bad that the secretaries gave up. In spite of this, the discussion continued. Each side accused the other of having surrendered copies of the Scriptures during the persecutions almost a century before. Augustine maintained that the Catholic Church was the true Church because it was to be found not only in Africa but throughout the Roman Empire. Fortunius maintained that his was the true Church because of the persecutions it had endured at the hands of the Catholics when large numbers of Donatists were killed, churches confiscated and bishops exiled. He insisted that Augustine answer the question whether the persecutor or the one persecuted was in the right. He challenged him to produce a single New Testament example of a righteous man killing someone else. Warming to the old man, who had stood up to him so well, Augustine earnestly asked for his help in ending the schism. 'The next day he came to me himself and we began to discuss the matter again, but I could not remain with him as the ordination of a bishop required my departure.'

6

The Preaching Magistrate

As a man left the church in Hippo someone asked him what was going on inside. 'The bishop is speaking', he answered. Week after week, year after year, many hundreds of people packed the church to hear Augustine. When he was a professor he had been a brilliant teacher and now he was a bishop he devoted himself unceasingly to the work of preaching. His sermons were biblical rambles: biblical, for they were exclusively concerned with the words of Scripture, with Christ and His Church, with Christian belief and behaviour; rambles, for they rarely fully explained any one text but passed quickly to many others drawn from all over the Bible, so that his talks were littered with hundreds of quotations. In this way his hearers acquired a knowledge of Scripture, for many could not read and very few possessed one of the bulky manuscripts of the Bible. He did not prepare the content of his messages in detail, nor keep to one subject, nor divide up his talks by clear headings, nor even tell Bible stories. His sermons were strictly pastoral, applying the word of God to the hearts of the people.

Like most of his contemporaries, including Jerome, he was more intent on drawing spiritual lessons out of Scripture than in establishing its original meaning, so that he often appeared to be a biblical magician who could produce gospel truth from the most unlikely passages. The five colonnades of the pool of Bethesda (John 5:1-7) he likened to the five books of Moses, the water in the pool to the Jews, and the troubling of the water to the sufferings of Christ. In his hands the fig tree under which Christ saw Nathanael (John 1:48) denoted his sins, for it reminded Augustine of the fig leaves with which Adam and Eve covered themselves after they had fallen. As for the sycamore Zacchaeus climbed, 'Ascend the tree where Jesus hung for you', he said, 'and *you* will see Jesus.' He could find mystic significance in Bible numbers: in 7, 8, or 10, in 40, 49, 50, 153, indeed in any number mentioned.

It would be easy to lengthen the list but quite wrong to imagine that because of such extravagances Augustine can be written off as a preacher of no significance, for a much larger collection of apt and powerful statements could be collected from his sermons. As he began to elucidate the seventh chapter of the Epistle to the Romans, he appealed to his huge audience, 'Give me a patient hearing so that if, because of the obscurity of the subject, I have a difficult exposition, I may at least have an easy speaking. If both are difficult, my labour will be great.' He then proceeded to give them a talk packed with Scripture to an extraordinary degree. 'It is one thing not to lust and another not to go after one's lusts. Not to lust is the state of one altogether perfect: not to go after his lusts is the state of one fighting. In no other way can you be perfect in this life than by knowing that you cannot be perfect in this life. I speak of myself as perfect and not perfect at the same time.'

He was so well acquainted with the lives of his hearers, their sorrows and their sins, that he was able to lace his sermons with allusions which riveted their attention. He described how some men, weary of their business by the end of the day, would try to finish quickly and get home to rest, while others so dreaded returning to the friction in their families that they wandered about outside. He referred to farmers sweating on the threshing floors in the summer heat and to labourers staggering under heavy loads, panting and thirsting, hoping there were not robbers ahead. He depicted wealthy people not daring to keep money at home for fear their servants found it, preferring the bank, 'where everything is well taken care of', and greedy men enlarging their property by moving back boundary stones at night. And he revealed that some people found it so hard to pay their bills that they would even ask the bishop's advice how best to get hold of other people's property. He illustrated his messages by alluding to 'maidens of God', girls who had renounced marriage for religious reasons but then had to face a father's anger and a mother's tears; to a man shivering in mid-winter because his mistress told him she preferred him in lighter clothes; and to a mother who softened little pieces of meat in her mouth before giving them to her infant son.

The church was so crowded that tempers were often frayed when fresh air was hard to come by and men trod on their neighbours' toes, but not everyone was really on Augustine's side. Many had already lost their hearts to the sporting heroes of the day, the charioteers. Others complained, 'I already live a good life. I commit no murder, no theft, no violence, no adultery, so why do I need Christ?' But they could all see his face and sense the appeal of his magnetic personality. 'Come, my brethren, catch my eagerness', he would say, and their response was often electric – 'your hearts I have not seen but I have heard your voices.'

He never curried their favour. 'If you are about to marry,' he urged them, 'keep yourselves for your wives. As you would have them come to you, so ought they to find you.' Having riveted their attention, he abruptly asked what good reasons they should have for not committing adultery and at once answered the question himself. 'Because you fear hell, you fear the punishment of eternal fire, you fear Christ's judgment, you fear the society of the devil, lest you be punished with him and burn with him. Fear by all means. You can fear nothing better.'

He did not find it easy work. 'My preaching almost always displeases me. I eagerly long for something better, the sense of which I often enjoy in my mind, but then I am grieved when I find that I cannot express it adequately in words.' On one occasion he admitted, 'I have suffered much toil and anxiety. I sympathized with you and was anxious for myself, but to my thinking the Lord has assisted both you and me. If with all my pains I have been tedious to any of you, I have finished, and I congratulate you that the whole Psalm has been expounded. In the very middle of it, fearing lest I should burden you, I was about to let you go.'

As the fourth century drew towards its close, prospects for peace in the Roman world were not good. The most powerful man in the Empire was a soldier of fortune named Stilicho, a Vandal from eastern Europe. The fate of the Romans rested in his hands at a time when various tribes of Germany and central Europe were pressing with mounting force upon the long rampart of the Rhine which had for so many centuries kept them at bay. By then Augustine had become a towering figure, whose knowledge and experience no one in Africa could match. Lesser men so hung upon his words that when he scribbled notes in the margin of his manuscript of Job someone got hold of it and distressed him by bringing them out as a book. Neither the clash of arms in Britain, nor slaughter on the Rhine, nor intrigues in Italy could disturb the tranquillity of lonely Hippo by the sea, backed by the Numidian mountains and the impenetrable Sahara.

As he worked at night in his study, or sat before the people massed in church, he could hear the waves breaking on the beach. Today the skeleton of Hippo, half-smothered in weeds and undergrowth, lies derelict on the edge of the Algerian town of Annaba, much of which was built on land reclaimed from the sea. In the fourth century the Mediterranean beat against the steep little hill now crowned by a museum. Hippo stretched along the shore where the road to Annaba airport runs, and inland to a higher hill on which an elaborate cathedral was erected by the French in the 1880s. Between Museum Hill and Cathedral Hill lie the bones of Hippo, partly buried under twenty feet of earth, partly excavated early in the twentieth century.

Close by Museum Hill was the church, able to take two thousand people standing. It is easy to see the actual spot in the centre of the apse where Augustine sat to preach on innumerable occasions. It takes only five minutes to walk round the block, treading on the huge stone slabs which were covering the central drain long before his day. In this block Augustine lived for much of his life, presiding over his group of dedicated celibates. Not far away lay the circular market and its adjacent shops, surrounded by extensive residential quarters with typically large Roman baths to north and south. Further inland stood the splendid forum with the theatre beyond it, utilising the steep slope of Cathedral Hill for its tiers of seats.

It was here in the last years of the fourth century that Augustine wrote the most famous of all his books, the *Confessions*, in which he told the story of his life up to his mother's death. At once extremely popular, it enables us to know him and Monica more intimately than most other figures in antiquity. At the same time he had already begun work on *The Trinity*, while a torrent of letters and shorter books flowed from his desk. Without parents to consider, with neither wife nor child to care for, he was able to devote his tremendous energy and exceptional talents to the needs of the people around him, to the city in which he was permanently anchored, and to the international Church he served. He took no holidays and had no leisure, yet he usually managed to preserve his health, speaking and writing with impressive freshness. His humility could also be impressive. 'So far am I from being acquainted with everything, that I read nothing in your letter with more sadness than this statement, both because it is manifestly untrue and because I am surprised you should not be aware that not only are many things unknown to me in countless other departments, but that even in the Scriptures themselves the things which I do not know are many more than the things which I know' (*Letter 55:38*).

Quite apart from the domestic and social problems brought before him daily in his capacity as an arbitrator, Augustine was never free from a maze of distressing situations plaguing the largely nominal Christian community of which he was the recognized head. A country congregation was in danger of being dragooned into accepting as their bishop a man who had already been officially deposed for misconduct. One of his colleagues began to read in church from books not in the accepted canon of Scripture. Some young men, tiring of his strictness, deserted his monastery and tried to get themselves ordained in Carthage on easier terms. Another monk complained of 'a vile proposal' made to him by a colleague.

In addition to coping with awkward people, Augustine grappled with problematical texts, including Christ's saying about the unforgivable sin, which he considered the most difficult in the whole Bible. For a long time he studied the problems it raised but deferred preaching on the subject, fearing that 'by words suggested at the moment' he might not do justice to his understanding of it. Then one Sunday he found himself listening to the twelfth chapter of Matthew in church. 'As the Gospel was being read,' he told the congregation, 'there was such a beating at my heart that I believed it was God's will you should hear something on the subject.' In the sermon which followed he refuted the popular idea that when a Christian, one who had received the Holy Spirit and been baptized, was afterwards guilty of adultery or murder, he had committed the unforgivable sin. Augustine insisted that in these cases there was always the possibility of repentance, followed by forgiveness. He then expounded his own view that the only unforgivable sin was impenitence, because the unrepentant man 'stops the source of forgiveness against himself', but he qualified it by pointing out that so long as the person is alive, hope remains. 'How do you know whether he may not be a Christian tomorrow?' So he defined the sin against the Holy Spirit as impenitence till death. But then he added a further qualification. In his opinion no sins could be forgiven outside the Catholic Church. From this he deduced that if someone who was not a Catholic repented of his sins but did not also repent of being 'an alien from the Church of God', his other repentance was of no profit to him and he was still guilty of the sin against the Holy Spirit.

7

The Truth is God Himself

God the Father

Augustine's normal way of referring to God was as the Creator. He rarely spoke of God the Father except when this was balanced by allusion to God the Son. But he called Him the Creator thousands of times, the Creator of the universe, the Creator of heaven and earth, the Creator of all Nature, the Creator of body and soul, the Creator of the mind, 'by whose laws the poles revolve, the stars fulfil their courses, the sun vivifies the day, the moon tempers the night: God, who maintains the framework, the mighty constancy of things, day after day by alternation of light and gloom, month after month by waxings and wanings of the moon, year after year by orderly succession of spring and summer and autumn and winter: God, above whom is nothing, beyond whom is nothing, without whom is nothing' (*Soliloquies* 4).

'Of all visible things the greatest is the world, of all invisible things the greatest is God. But the existence of the world is a matter of observation; the existence of God is a matter of belief. For the belief that God made the world we can have no more trustworthy witness than God Himself. Where do we hear this witness? Nowhere more clearly than in the Holy Scriptures where His prophet said, 'In the beginning God made heaven and earth'. Are we to suppose the prophet was there when God made them? No, but the Wisdom of God was there and that Wisdom passes into holy souls and tells them soundlessly the story of God's works. He has given us the existence we share with stones, the reproductive life we share with plants, the life of the senses we share with animals, and the life of the intellect shared only with angels. We can never give Him adequate thanks for our sight of sky and earth, or our possession of intelligence and reason, which enable us to search for Him who created all those things' (*City 5:11, 11:2,4*).

'God willed to create the first man in His own image as a new act of creation, surpassing all living creatures in virtue of reason and intelligence. The whole human race took its beginning from that one man. There is nothing in the whole of creation so near to Him in nature. When He created the woman who was to be joined with the man, He made her out of the man, so that the whole human race should spread out from the one original man. No faithful Christian should doubt that anyone who is born anywhere derives from that one first-created human being. This is true however extraordinary others may appear to us in bodily shape, colour, language, or in any other way' (*City 12:9, 15, 22*).

'Some people regard the account of our creation as fable not fact. Because it is beyond their own experience they adopt a critical attitude. If we did not know that monkeys, long-tailed apes and chimpanzees are only animals, some naturalists might pass them off on us as human beings and get away with such nonsense' (*City 12:24* and *16:8*). He acknowledged that allegorical interpretations of the Garden of Eden in the book of Genesis might be valid 'provided we also believe in the truth of the story as a faithful record of historical fact' (*City 13:21*).

He often alluded to changes taking place in animals, trees and other things which lack intelligence, sense and life. 'We see a constant succession as some pass away and others arise, as the weaker succumb to the stronger and those that are overwhelmed change into the qualities of their conquerors. Thus we have a world of continual transience. Those that have not been given an eternal existence obey the laws of the Creator, changing in accordance with the lines of development He has laid down for them in the scheme of things' (*City 12:4-5*). 'Just as the seed of a tree contains invisibly all the things that will in time develop into the tree, so the world itself contained all those things which would arise in the course of time in the way we now know them, through those operations which God carries on even till now' (*Gen. 5:23:45*). 'Seeds visible to our eyes are quite distinct from the hidden seeds from which, at the bidding of the Creator, the earth produced the first buds and living creatures. Their power of production was not exhausted at that time. Suitable combinations of circumstances were needed, enabling them to burst forth and complete their species' (*Trinity 3:8:13-14*).

'The elements of the physical world have a fixed power and quality, determining for each thing what it can or cannot do. Thus a bean does not come from a grain of wheat, nor wheat from a bean. Humans do not come from animals, nor animals from humans. Over this whole course of nature is the power of the Creator. In the course of time He does with each thing what He originally made possible in it: this plant grows one way and another plant another way: a human being can speak and an animal cannot. Not even He would do in them what He Himself predetermined was impossible to be done in them' (*Gen. 9:17:32*).

So the evolution he envisaged was an outworking of creation, a later stage of what God had initiated. And, in spite of his acute sense of the horrors of history and 'the disasters of modern times', he had no doubt that 'God is the Governor of the universe. He is in control as the master of events, even to the

wind-blown leaves of the trees. He rules everything He created'
(*City 4:33, 9:13, Confessions 7:6*). Romans 11:36 was
fundamental to his understanding of the faith, 'From Him and
through Him and to Him are all things'.

> 'He is so permanent, so mysterious,
> never new, never old, making all things new,
> ever in action, ever at rest,
> my God, my life, my sacred delight,
> Father of Truth, Father of Wisdom,
> Father of the true and crowning life,
> from whom to be turned away is to fall,
> to whom to be turned back is to rise again,
> in whom to abide is to stand firm.
> God, through whom we overcome the enemy,
> God, by whom we flee evil and follow good,
> God, through whom we yield not to calamities,
> God, through whom death is swallowed up in victory,
> hear me, graciously hear me,
> open my eyes, drive delusion from me,
> receive, I pray, Your fugitive,
> to You I feel I must return.'
> (*Confessions 1:4, Soliloquies 1:2-6*)

God the Son
Augustine continually referred to the Lord Jesus Christ as our
Saviour, yet his favourite title for Him was 'the Mediator', so he
quoted 1 Timothy 2:5-6a hundreds of times, 'There is one God
and one Mediator between God and humanity, the man Christ
Jesus, who gave Himself a ransom for all.'

'Such a Mediator should have something in common with God and something in common with us. If he were in both parts like us, he would be too far from God. If he were in both parts like God, he would be too far from us. Christ is not a Mediator because He is equal with the Father, for in this respect He is as far distant from us as the Father is, so the apostle does not say, "There is one Mediator, even Jesus Christ' but his words are "the man Christ Jesus". He is Mediator in that He is man' (*Confessions 10:42* and *Original Sin 2:33*).

Of this theme Augustine never wearied, epitomising it with impressive simplicity by quoting Christ's words, 'As the Father has loved me, so have I loved you' (John 15:9) and pointing out that 'When He says "The Father... me... you", He is alluding to Himself as Mediator.'

Sometimes he confirmed it from his own experience: 'I set about finding a way to enjoy You, but I could not find it till I embraced the Mediator, the man Christ Jesus, who called to me saying, "I am the way, the truth and the life". When sin had placed a wide gulf between God and the human race, it was expedient that a Mediator, – who alone was born, lived and died without sin – should reconcile us to God, that our pride might be exposed and cured through His humility, that we might be shown how far we had departed from God, that an example might be given us in His life of obedience, that a guarantee of the resurrection of the body might be seen in the resurrection of the Redeemer, and that in His person the devil might be subdued' (*Enchiridion 108*).

Thanks to his success in tempting Adam and Eve, as Augustine frequently emphasized, 'the devil had possession of the human race, ruling in their hearts, deceiving and enslaving them' (*Tractate 52:6*). It was in the context of this bondage that he commonly presented the good news of the coming of a

Saviour.

'What shall I say of His Cross? The blood of Christ, poured out for the forgiveness of our sins, was given as a price for us, that we might be freed' (*Trinity 13:15:19*). He constantly linked the Cross to Isaiah 53, Psalm 22, 1 Peter 2:24 'He Himself bore our sins in His body on the cross', and to Christ's statement 'This is my blood which is shed for many for the forgiveness of sins'. 'Christ, though guiltless, took our punishment that He might cancel our guilt and do away with our punishment. These are not my conjectures, but are constantly affirmed by the Apostle Paul. Christ bore the curse for us. The real death into which the serpent cast us by his fatal counsel was hung on the Cross' (*Faustus 14:4* and *7*).

Quoting 2 Corinthians 5:21, 'God made Him, who had no sin, to be sin for us', he asked 'How do we tolerate this, that Christ Himself should be sin? This passage does not seem to me more fittingly understood than that Christ was made a sacrifice for sin and on this account was called "sin". He took away death by death and sin by sin' (*Sermon 84:5, Original Sin 3:6*). 'By faith in Christ, His death and resurrection, and His blood, thousands of believers are delivered from the dominion of the devil. Even the Cross itself is a judgment seat. The Judge was set in the middle. One thief who believed was delivered, the other who reviled was condemned. Already He signified what He will do with the living and the dead' (*Tractate 52:6, 31:11*).

God the Holy Spirit

He acknowledged that the Holy Spirit had to a certain extent been active in the Old Testament prophets and in John the Baptist, but 'The sending of the Holy Spirit after the glorification of Christ was unique. Nowhere else do we read that people spoke in languages they did not know through the Holy Spirit coming upon them. This was to show that the whole world, all nations with their different languages, would believe in Christ through the gift of the Holy Spirit' (*Trinity 4:20:29*).

He does not seem to dwell on the tongues mentioned in I Corinthians 12-14, though he admirably surveys the variety of the Spirit's gifts: 'This man has one gift and that man another, and what that man has this man does not have' (*Tractate 14:10*).

He often quoted I Corinthians 13:1, 'If I speak in the languages of men and of angels but have not love', in order to stress that the fruit of the Spirit is primarily love: 'What languages could have been wanting to Paul, who said, "I speak with tongues more than you all'? What is more sublime than the gift of languages? Yet if you take away love it is a gong, a clanging cymbal' (*Proceedings 32, Sermon 92:9*). He was asked whether a baptized believer who does not speak the languages of all nations has perhaps not received the Holy Spirit: 'God forbid that our hearts should be tempted by such faithlessness. The reason why no one speaks in the languages of all nations is that the Church itself now does so. Before, when the Church was only in one nation, it spoke in the languages of all, signifying what was to come to pass' (*Tractate 32:7*). So when he was asked whether he himself spoke in tongues, he replied: 'Clearly I do. Every tongue is mine' (*Tractate 32:7*).

The Trinity
'The Trinity is not three Gods but one God. The Father is God and the Son is God and the Holy Spirit is God, and all three together are one God, although the Father is not the Son, the Son is not the Father, and the Holy Spirit is neither the Father nor the Son. Through the mere necessity of speaking it is lawful to say "three Persons", because Scripture does not contradict

it, whereas if we were to say "three Gods" Scripture would contradict it' (*Trinity 1:4:7* and *15:17:28-32*).

'The Trinity works indivisibly in everything. Nothing is done by the Father which is not also done by the Son and by the Holy Spirit. Nothing is done by the Son which is not also done by the Father and by the Holy Spirit. Nothing is done by the Holy Spirit which is not also done by the Father and by the Son. Yet the Father does some things, the Son other things, and the Holy Spirit yet others. In that highest Trinity one is as much as the three together. Each is in each and all in each, and each in all, and all in all, and all are one' (*Trinity 1:4:7, 4:21:30, 6:10:12* and *Letter 11:2-3*).

He insisted that statements in Scripture which do not specifically mention the Holy Spirit should not be thought to imply His exclusion. 'The harmony within the Trinity must be understood, even though it is not mentioned' (*Trinity 6:9:10*). And this important principle he also applied when the Father or the Son are not specifically mentioned. 'The Holy Spirit is sometimes mentioned as if He alone sufficed for our blessedness. And He does alone so suffice, because He cannot be divided from the Father and the Son. He is specially called the Spirit of the Father and the Spirit of the Son. He will not come without them, nor they without Him' (*Trinity 1:8:18*).

At times he had to resist those who maintained that 'the Holy Spirit is greater than the Son'. 'Let them wake up if they can. The Holy Spirit glorifies the Son, whom the Father also glorifies, but it is not written that the Holy Spirit Himself is glorified either by the Father or by the Son' (*Trinity 1:8:18* and *2:4:6*). And he had to cope with ardent believers who felt that, having received the Holy Spirit, no human teacher was necessary, and who doubted whether those who had not had a like experience to the apostles on the day of Pentecost were true

Christians at all. 'No, No. Let us put away false pride and learn whatever can be learnt from others, lest being ensnared by the wiles of the enemy and our own perversity we may even refuse to go to the churches to hear the gospel or read a book. Let us beware of such dangerous temptations' (*Doctrine: Preface 5*).

8

Baptism, Communion and the Sabbath

Baptism

Throughout his writings Augustine maintained that baptism imparts to us the forgiveness of sins, frees us from the defilement of original sin, and opens to us the door of heaven. 'We are born again through Christ in baptism.' So he approved the custom of calling baptism simply 'salvation'. He insisted that 'there is no one who in baptism does not die to sin. Infants die only to original sin. Those who are older die also to all the sins they have added to the sin they brought with them. Just as real as Christ's death, so real is the forgiveness of our sins' (*Forgiveness I:23, 34, Enchiridion 42, 43, 52*).

He considered that the efficacy of baptism was not only retrospective. 'By this sacrament of regeneration all evils are cleansed, including those committed afterwards, so that baptism is not to be repeated as often as sin is repeated. For the sake of light sins, without which we cannot live, we are provided with the prayer, "Forgive us our sins". Once for all we have washing in baptism; every day we have washing in prayer. The Lord's Prayer is our daily cleansing. A person who has already been baptized is never to be baptized again. By a sort of hidden instinct from heaven people shrink from anyone who has received it twice' (*Marriage I:38*).

He repeatedly stressed the necessity of infant baptism, quoting from the closing verses of Mark's Gospel, 'Whoever believes and is baptized will be saved, but whoever does not believe will be condemned.' 'Who can be unaware that, in the case of infants, being baptized is to believe and not being baptized is not to believe? They perish if they are not baptized. By the answer of those through whose agency they are born again, carried by pious hands to Jesus Christ the Saviour, the Spirit of righteousness transfers to them that faith, which of their own will they could not yet have, and regenerates them in Christ as believers. Let no eternal salvation be promised to infants without baptism, for none is promised in the Scriptures' (*City 21:14, Forgiveness 1:39, 55*).

Now and again, however, Augustine warned that a baptized person might prove to have received God's grace in vain. 'Who does not know that baptized infants fail to benefit from what they received as little children if, on coming to years of reason, they fail to believe and abstain from unlawful desires? Anyone who desires to escape from everlasting pains needs not only to be baptized but to pass from the devil to Christ. What does the fact of baptism profit people if they are not made righteous? It is true that Christ said, "No one can enter the kingdom of God unless born of water and the Spirit", but did He not also say, "Unless your righteousness exceeds that of the Scribes and Pharisees you will not enter the kingdom of heaven"? Renovation only begins with the forgiveness of sins. Since we still need to be renewed inwardly day by day, we are not as yet wholly renewed. Even after having been baptized we are still in some degree in our old condition, still children of the world. It was those already baptized whom the apostle exhorted to put off the old and put on the new, an exhortation which would have been unsuitable if the perfect change had already taken place. Though full forgiveness of sins takes place in baptism, character does not at once undergo a total change' (*Forgiveness 2:9* and *44*).

In his struggle to reconcile the assertions of the New Testament with his daily experience of human perversity he went so far as to admit: 'It is not easy to say what is the precise value of the sacrament. It is complete in itself, yet no one can receive salvation without amendment of life. The word of God is not silent nor is it lenient: it says openly that those who lead a wicked life have no part in the kingdom of God. The sacrament of baptism is one thing, the conversion of the heart is another: salvation is made complete through the two together. Baptism may exist when conversion of the heart is wanting, and conversion may be found when baptism has not been received' (*Baptism 4:23:31, 4:18:26, 4:25:31*).

He was prepared to admit that in cases where it was impossible for baptism to be administered, 'faith and conversion of heart' might take its place (*Baptism 4:22:30, 4:23:31*).

Communion
'The Churches of Christ maintain it to be an inherent principle that without baptism and partaking of the Lord's Supper it is impossible for any one to attain to the kingdom of God and everlasting life' (*Forgiveness 1:34*).

Augustine employed no one term to denote Holy Communion. He often called it the Eucharist or the Lord's Supper, but most frequently just 'the sacrament'. 'Was not Christ once for all offered up in His own person as a sacrifice? And yet is He not likewise offered up in the sacrament as a sacrifice not only in the special solemnities of Easter but also daily among our congregations? What is placed on the altar of God is Christ' (*Letter 98:9, Tractate 45:9*). His countless references to this subject were influenced not so much by the accounts in the Synoptic Gospels and I Corinthians II as by John 6:47-58, where the words 'Whoever eats my flesh and drinks my blood has eternal life' are repeated with impressive force.

However, he disapproved of 'merely eating the body and blood of Christ in the sacrament, as many evil people do', for he wanted to see a more intelligent approach: 'To understand it according to the flesh is death. To eat Christ's body and to drink His blood in reality is to live in Christ so that Christ lives in you. It needs to be visibly celebrated, but it must be spiritually understood' (*Tractate 26:11, City 21:25, Psalms 99:8*). So, 'do not get your mouth ready but your heart' (*Sermon 62:5*).

Time and again he insisted that 'Christ bore Himself in His hands when He said, "This is my body". The bread you see on the altar is the body of Christ as soon as it is sanctified by God's word. What is contained in the chalice is the blood of Christ as soon as it is sanctified by God's word' (*Psalms 33:1*).

When asked how often one should take the Eucharist, Augustine refused to give a precise ruling. He considered it one of those issues which 'do not admit of final decision by the authority of Holy Scripture, or by the tradition of the Universal Church, or by manifestly good influence on morals. In some places no day passes without the sacrifice being offered, in others it is only on Saturday and the Lord's Day, or it may be only on the Lord's Day' (*Letter 54:2:2-3*).

'It is clear that when the disciples first received the body and blood of the Lord they had not been fasting. Must we then censure the Universal Church because the sacrament is everywhere taken fasting? Certainly not, for from that time it pleased the Holy Spirit to appoint that the body of the Lord should take precedence over all other food' (*Letter 54:6:8*).

Occasionally Augustine mentions 'commemorating the souls of the pious dead at the altar of God at the time of partaking of the body of Christ' (*City 20:9*): 'The souls of the dead are benefited by the piety of their living friends who offer the sacrifice of the Mediator on their behalf, but these services are of advantage only to those who during their lives have earned such merit that they can help them. In the case of the very bad, even though they do not assist the dead, they are a species of consolation to the living. Where they are profitable, their benefit consists either in making a full remission of sins, or at least in making the condemnation more tolerable' (*Enchiridion 110*). He quoted no Scripture in support of such ideas.

******

The Sabbath

'God proclaims to us a Sabbath. What sort of Sabbath? A Sabbath in the heart. A Sabbath within. Jews observe the Sabbath in a carnal manner by physical rest. They abstain from labour. Our rest is from evil deeds' (*Psalms 92:2*).

Augustine's views on this subject are most significant:

1. He knows nothing of a weekly day of rest.
2. What we call Sunday, he calls the Lord's Day.
3. He never calls the Lord's Day the Sabbath.
4. He never applies to the Lord's Day what the Old Testament says about observing the Sabbath.

'Of all the Ten Commandments that which related to the Sabbath was the only one in which the thing commanded was typical, a figure of the spiritual rest to which we are invited by the Lord Himself in the words "Come unto me all you who labour and are heavy laden and I will give you rest" (Matt. 11:28). All the other commandments we are to obey. They are devoid of mystical meaning and are to be literally observed. But we are not commanded to observe the Sabbath day by literally resting from physical labour, as the Jews do' (*Letter 55:12:22*).

In many a memorable saying he summarized his standpoint: 'When we find rest in Him we truly observe the Sabbath' (*Answer 2:3*). 'The Christian observes the Sabbath by abstaining from sin' (*Tractate 3:19*). 'We have our Sabbath in Him' (*Faustus 19:9*).

He never suggested that the observance of the Sabbath has been superseded by the observance of what we call Sunday, but he frequently asserted that Heaven is its fulfilment. 'That will be the greatest of Sabbaths, the Sabbath that has no evening, our Sabbath, the Sabbath of everlasting life' (*City 22:30, Confessions 13:36*).

9

The Bible Never Lies

Having been rescued and transformed by what he read in Paul's Epistle to the Romans, Augustine remained throughout life an enthusiastic champion of the Bible. It was his intention that everything he preached or wrote should be 'either what I found stated in Scripture or what I could infer from it'. He was convinced that 'the Bible never lies' (*City II:6*).

'In expounding to you the Holy Scriptures I, as it were, break bread for you. What I deal out to you is not my own. What you eat, I eat. What you live on, I live on. We have a common storehouse in heaven, for that is where the word of God comes from' (*Sermon 45:1*).

'Holy Scripture brings a remedy for the terrible diseases of the human will. God in his goodness has provided the sacred writings to mould our characters and to guide us from this world of wickedness to the blessed world above' (*Doctrine 2:5:6* and *4:6:10*).

'Jesus Christ the Mediator spoke in former times through the prophets, later through His own mouth, then through the apostles. He also instituted the canonical Scriptures in which we put our trust concerning what we need to know for our good and yet are incapable of discovering for ourselves' (*City II:3*).

He had not easily adopted this attitude. It was the outcome of prolonged intellectual struggle which enabled him to resist the intense hostility of Faustus, the Manichean bishop described in the *Confessions*, a formidable opponent, whose doubts have been echoed over more than a thousand years.

Faustus said to him: 'You ask if I believe in the Old Testament. Of course not, for I do not keep its precepts. Neither, I imagine, do you. I reject circumcision as disgusting and, if I mistake not, so do you. I reject the observance of Sabbaths as superfluous. I suppose you do the same. I do not mix Christian newness with Hebrew oldness. The Old Testament promises riches, children, long life and the land of Canaan, but only to the circumcised, the Sabbath observers, those offering sacrifices and abstaining from pork. I pay no attention to these things, as being trifling and useless for the salvation of the soul. The Jews, satisfied with the Old Testament, reject the New, and we who have received the New Testament from Christ, reject the Old. You receive both, and the one is not completed by the other but corrupted.'

Faustus accepted the New Testament, but claimed the right to question the genuineness of any particular statement in it. 'I am taught to believe that many things which pass under the name of the Saviour are spurious, for the Gospels were not written by Christ or his apostles but compiled long afterwards and published under the names of apostles to give an appearance of authority to all these rumours and falsehoods. Yet you receive everything without examination, condemning the use of reason, which is the prerogative of human nature.'

Forced to grapple with such a competent opponent, Augustine compiled a massive volume dealing with every criticism Faustus had made. 'It is clearly your aim to deprive Scripture of all authority and to make every individual's mind the judge of what passage in it is to be approved and what rejected. This is not to be subject to Scripture but to make Scripture subject to you' (*Faustus 32:19*).

In this task he had to search his own heart too: 'I began to consider the countless things I believed which had happened with me not there – historical matters, facts about places I had never visited, information given me by doctors – and unless we accepted these things we should do nothing at all in this life. Most strongly of all it struck me how firmly I believed I was born of a particular father and mother, which I could only know on the word of others. Thus God brought me to see that I must not give heed to those who said to me, "How do you know that those Scriptures were given to us by the Spirit of the one true God?" How do we know the authorship of the works of Plato, Aristotle or Cicero except by the transmission of the information from one to another? How can we be sure of the authorship of any book if we doubt the apostolic authorship of those books attributed to the apostles by the Church which the apostles themselves founded?' (*Confessions 6:5, Faustus 33:6.*)

He strongly denied that he condemned the use of reason, though experience had taught him that 'people cannot be restrained from sins by reason' and that 'when we come to divine things reason turns away, for it cannot see clearly' (*Profit 9, Morals 7*). 'If reason be found contradicting Scripture, it only deceives by a semblance of truth. On the other hand if, against the most manifest testimony of reason, anything be set up claiming to have the authority of the Holy Scriptures, he who does this is misapprehending what he has read and is setting up against the truth not the real meaning of Scripture, which he has failed to discover, but an opinion of his own' (*Letter 143:7*).

Augustine frequently reflected on the relationship between the Old Testament and the New Testament, convinced that: 'The word of God is a two-edged sword' (*City 20:21*).

'Let us not follow those who think the two Testaments are

contrary to each other. These books are in perfect harmony, for what is the Old Testament but a concealed form of the New, and what is the New Testament but the revelation of the Old? What is latent in the former is patent in the latter' (*Sermon 32:8-9, City 5:18, 16:26*). 'For those who rightly understand it, the Old Testament is a prophecy of the New. Under the Old Testament the secret of the kingdom of heaven was veiled, obscured in the disguise of earthly promises, but in the New Testament the truth was revealed that there is another life, for which this life ought to be disregarded' (*Faustus 22:76*).

He perpetually contrasted the eternal blessings of the new covenant with the temporal rewards and worldly felicity of the old (*City 18:35*). So he did not hesitate to refer to 'the Jewish Scriptures' (*City 18:47*), 'the sacred Scriptures of the Hebrews' (*City 19:26*), illuminated in the fullness of time by: 'the sacred books which are the special property of us Christians, not shared by us with the Hebrews' (*City 20:24*).

He therefore admitted that the New Testament was more valuable than the Old, and that Christians are 'sons of the New Testament'. 'Although the Old Testament is prior in time, the New Testament is to be put before the Old Testament in order of importance, for the Old is the herald of the New. It was Jesus Christ Himself who said that a scribe instructed in the kingdom of heaven brings out of his storeroom 'things new and old' (Matt. 13:52), not 'old and new' which He obviously would have said had He not preferred to observe the order of value rather than the order of time' (*City 20:4*).

******

Like Christians in other ages, Augustine had to consider different translations of the Bible. In the third century B.C. the Old

Testament had been translated from Hebrew into Greek. Traditionally achieved by seventy scholars, this famous translation, frequently quoted in the New Testament, has always been known as the Septuagint. 'From this Septuagint a translation was made into Latin which the Latin-speaking churches retain, although our time has produced the presbyter Jerome, a man of great learning, master of all three languages. He has translated the Old Testament into Latin, not from the Greek but from the Hebrew, and the Jews acknowledge his accuracy' (*City 18:43*).

He was aware of the problem that the Septuagint – and so, of course, the Latin translated from it – differed from the Hebrew with mysterious frequency. His solution to this dilemma was to maintain: 'The very same Spirit that was in the prophets when they uttered their messages was also at work in the seventy scholars when they translated them. Both sources should be employed as authoritative. Both are inspired by God. In this even I, in my small measure, follow the apostles, because they quote from both sources, the Hebrew and the Septuagint' (*City 18:43-44*).

The Latin Bible Augustine had inherited included the Old Testament Apocrypha. Though admitting that 'writings not included in the Jewish canon do not carry so much weight', he frequently quoted *The Wisdom of Solomon* and *Ecclesiasticus* (*City 17:20*).

To the end of his life he continued to wrestle with the Bible, admitting that 'even our probing of the Scriptures is laborious' (*City 11:31*). His comment on 2 Thessalonians 2:6-7 was 'I confess that the meaning of this completely escapes me.' An important matter which he clarified as he matured was Christ's statement 'On this rock, I will build my church' in Matthew 16:18. Early on he had at times suggested that Peter himself was the rock, but later he always taught that the church was built on the faith Peter had just confessed in saying 'You are the Christ, the Son of the living God', which he liked to connect with Paul's words in I Corinthians 10:4, 'that rock was Christ'. So he insisted 'Christ said to Peter, "I will build you upon Myself, not Myself upon you." Men who wished to be built upon men said "I follow Paul and I Apollos and I Peter", but others said "I follow Christ" (I Cor. 1:12). What Christ said to Peter was "You are Peter" (Matt. 16:18) not "You are Rock". The Rock was Christ' (*Sermon 26:1, Tractate 124:4, Homily 10:1*).

10

The Moral Battle

'This present life of ours is evidence of the terrifying abyss of ignorance in which we are all engulfed', Augustine declared in dictating the closing chapters of *The City of God.* In addition to hatred, war, fraud, theft, murder, violence, cruelty and savagery, he listed the sexual vices of 'lust, indecency, promiscuity, fornication, adultery, incest and unnatural vice in women as well as men, disgusting acts too filthy to be named. Left to ourselves we would fall into all or most of these sins and crimes' (*City 22:22*). The allusion to unnatural vice was his unvarying attitude to homosexuality, which he regarded as a satanic temptation, 'an uncleanness which it is shameful even to mention' (*Enchiridion 78*). 'Males burning against males' (*Against Lying 34*) reminded him of the 'effeminates, public perverts', whom he had seen begging on the streets of Carthage, and of 'the Apostle's attack on the horrible vices of women who changed to practices contrary to nature' (*City 14:23*). 'When people get accustomed to them, even detestable sins are looked upon as trivial or not as sins at all, so that they are boasted about and published far and wide. And so in our own times many forms of sin are so openly and habitually practised that not only dare we not excommunicate a layman, we dare not even degrade a clergyman for the commission of them, though they are so great that the kingdom of God is wholly shut against them' (*Enchiridion 80*).

He faced an uphill task in advocating righteousness to his hearers in Hippo:

'Many people in the Church are liars, wrongdoers, adulterers, drunkards, extortioners, slave-traders, addicted to black arts and other vices contrary to the teaching of Christ and the word of God. If one begins to reprove them they ask, "Why then did God make me like this?" Instead of correcting their behaviour, they love their sins and accuse their Maker. Sometimes they even threaten to take legal action' (*Homily 3:9*).

The pursuit of virtue was a constant theme in his preaching and books. Paul's contrast between the works of the flesh and the fruit of the Spirit was never far from his mind. He spoke movingly about 'the war in which we are engaged', the moral battle all Christians had to fight. 'Sharper is the fight of the young: I know it well, I have passed through it' (*Sermon 78:11*).

He knew he needed to speak strongly against drunkenness and 'that frightful temptation', the thirst for revenge, when anger grips the mind and bursts out in abuse, blows and kicks (*Sermon 57:11, Tractate 41:12*): 'Pride is the source of all sins. Pride does its own will, humility does the will of God' (*Tractate 25:16*).

And he never tired of stressing that it is only 'in so far as the life that proceeds from our being born of God is flourishing within us that we are righteous' (*Correction 9:40*), and of warning his hearers that 'The word of God is neither silent nor lenient. It says openly that those who lead a wicked life have no part in the kingdom of God' (*Baptism 4:18:26*).

Augustine did his best to achieve a balance between the possibility of living righteously and the continuing imperfection of all Christians, including himself. 'Our present righteousness is by faith, but it will not be perfected in us until the struggle with flesh and blood is over, and death has been swallowed up in victory. At present we are still fighting. If you fight the devil alone you will be overcome, but with God you can overcome the devil' (*Homily 4:3* and *4:8*).

'In this immense forest of snares and perils, I have thrust many sins out of my heart, but, with so many things buzzing about our daily life on every side, would I dare to say that nothing can draw me to look at it or through vain curiosity to desire it?' (*Confessions 10:35.*) He was particularly ashamed that in his dreams he was sometimes guilty of indiscretions which in real life he would have resisted: 'Upon waking I discover that I did not commit the act, though I grieve that in some way or other it was done in me. Is not your hand powerful, O God Almighty, to prevent such a thing, winning the chaste mind even in sleep, even when I am in the prime of life? But now I confess what I still am in this way of evil, grieving that I am not yet made perfect' (*Confessions 10:30*).

The majority of people massed before him in church were married men. 'In conjugal fidelity you must bear with everything, however annoying it may be. If any one has a wife who is barren, blind, deaf, lame, or worn out by disease, pain, or something horrible – but not adultery – let him endure it for the sake of his plighted love. Let him not only not put away such a wife but, even if he cannot have her, let him not marry someone else however beautiful, healthy or rich. Any other unlawful embrace would be even worse. Let him flee fornication and unworthy behaviour of any kind. Let him maintain his Christian morals, whatever bad habits rise up against him' (*Mount 1:18:54*). He was asked whether a Christian would be guilty of adultery if, his wife being barren or unwilling for intercourse, he took another woman with her permission, as Abraham took Hagar with Sarah's consent. 'An example is indeed found in the Old Testament. But the human race has now reached greater precepts. Such an opinion is not to be entertained' (*Mount 1:16:49*).

He had stern words for people whose morals were

disreputable but who thought they were safe because they were good Catholics. 'What does baptism profit anyone if he is not made righteous? We must be on our guard to make sure we are not deceived by clever talk into believing evil to be good or good evil, lest hostility provoke us into returning evil for evil, or immoderate sadness overwhelm us, or an unthankful heart make us sluggish in doing acts of kindness. We must watch against the danger that sin makes us obey our bodies' cravings, that our eyes may be the servants of our desires, that our imagination may dwell on wrongful delights, that we may listen with pleasure to indecent talk, that our liking and not God's law may govern our actions, that in this conflict we should expect to win in our own strength instead of by the grace of Him who gives us the victory though our Lord Jesus Christ' (*City 21:27, 22:23*).

He was capable of presenting other aspects of righteousness with remarkable force, as he did when preaching on what Christ had to say about the sheep and the goats at the last judgment in Matthew 25:31-46: 'This passage in the Scriptures much astonishes me and I ought repeatedly to call your attention to it. At the end of the world Christ will say to those on His right, "Receive the kingdom" and to those on His left, "Depart from me into the eternal fire". Why will the first receive the kingdom? Because, "I was hungry and you gave me food." Why will the others go into eternal fire? Because, "I was hungry and you gave me nothing to eat." Now, I ask, what does this mean? He did not say, "Receive the kingdom, for you have lived chastely, not been drunkards, oppressed no one, deceived no one". All He said was, "I was hungry and you gave me food". The Lord made no mention of the rest, only of this. And He did not blame the ungodly for being adulterers, murderers, cheats, or unbelievers. All He said was, "I was hungry and you gave me nothing to eat". I see that you are as surprised as I am. It is indeed remarkable. I search out as best as I can the reason for these strange sayings, and I will not conceal it from you. Repentance for sins changes people for the better, but it does not seem as though it will profit you without merciful deeds. It was John the Baptist who said, "Produce fruit in keeping with repentance. Every tree that does not produce good fruit will be cut down and thrown into the fire". No one, then, who does not produce such fruit should think that he will attain pardon for his sins by a barren repentance. When they asked John what this good fruit was, he replied, "the man who has two coats should share with him who has none and the one who has food should do the same". What could be plainer than that? What will it profit you to pray for forgiveness if you don't produce fruit in keeping with repentance? You would be cast into the fire! So, if you want to be heard when you pray for pardon, "Give, and it will be given to you" (Luke 6:38). If this be good counsel, let us not be slow in taking heed to it' (*Sermon 10:8-11*).

11

Jerome: Scholar and Linguist

Soon after moving to Hippo, Augustine had started
corresponding with Jerome, the greatest Christian scholar of
the age, who was twenty-three years older than he was, at this
stage spending the last years of his life at Bethlehem, pouring
out a stream of Bible translations and commentaries. He had
already embarked on the titanic task of producing a new
translation of the Old Testament from the original Hebrew
which, along with a revision of the Gospels, was to form the
basis of a new Latin Bible, in due time to be known as the
Vulgate. Augustine however, not adequately aware of Jerome's
greatness and prodigious learning, urged him to put Greek Bible
commentaries into Latin rather than produce a fresh Latin
version, and expressed his surprise that anything useful could
be discovered in Hebrew Old Testament manuscripts which
had escaped previous translators. He also questioned some
points in Jerome's commentaries, even accusing him of not
really being convinced of the truth of the Scriptures. He sent
copies of his letter to people in various countries, but
unfortunately the original was lost when the man taking it to
Bethlehem died. So a year or more passed before someone
showed a copy to Jerome, who could hardly be blamed for his
distress that such criticisms had become widely known. 'Do
not, because you are young', he wrote, 'challenge a veteran in
the field of Scripture. I have had my time and run my course to
the utmost of my strength. It is but fair that I should rest, while

you in your turn run.'

When Jerome's letter arrived, Augustine sat down to answer it in troubled mood. 'It remains for me to confess as I now do, my fault as having been the first to offend by writing that letter, which I cannot deny to be mine. I therefore entreat you by the mercy of Christ to forgive me wherein I have injured you.' Realising at last what kind of man Jerome really was, he longed to sit beside him and learn from him. 'I have not now, and I can never hope to have, such knowledge of the Divine Scriptures as I see you possess', he confessed. 'Whatever abilities I may have for such study, I devote entirely to the instruction of the people whom God has entrusted to me and I am wholly precluded by my ecclesiastical occupations from having leisure for any further prosecution of my studies than is necessary for my duties in public teaching.'

Their letters continued to cross. The great translator, by then aged seventy-three, whose monumental Latin Bible was about to be given to the world, was not a little perplexed to know how to cope with his correspondent in Africa. 'You are sending me letter upon letter,' he complained, 'challenging an old man, disturbing the peace of one who asks only to be allowed to be silent, and you seem to desire to display your learning.' He aptly described Augustine's original letter as 'a honeyed sword'. A friend of his had come across a copy of it on an island in the Adriatic. 'The same letter is reported to be in the possession of most of the Christians in Rome and throughout Italy, and has come to everyone but myself, to whom alone it was ostensibly sent.' He felt Augustine had set at nought the laws of brotherly fellowship and regretted that the world should see them quarrelling like children. 'It does not become me, who have spent my life from youth until now sharing the arduous labours of pious brethren in an obscure monastery, to presume to write anything against a bishop of my own communion, especially against one whom I had begun to love before I knew him, who also sought my friendship before I sought his, and whom I rejoiced to see rising as a successor to myself in the careful study of the Scriptures. Farewell, my very dear friend, my son in years, my father in ecclesiastical dignity. And to this I most particularly request your attention, that henceforth you make sure that I be the first to receive whatever you may write to me.'

Shortly afterwards another man came from Bethlehem with a further letter from Jerome. 'Our armour is Christ', he declared, marshalling many a scriptural quotation before getting down to business. 'I say nothing of the compliments by which you attempt to take the edge off your censure.' Then, with great vigour and remarkable command both of the biblical text and of earlier commentaries on it, he defended his views and in return charged Augustine with error in his understanding of Paul's attitude to the Mosaic Law. He appealed to him to 'refrain from stirring up against me the unlearned crowd, who esteem you as their bishop and regard with the respect due to the priestly office the orations which you deliver in the church, but who esteem lightly a decrepit old man like me'. He proceeded with unerring aim to demolish Augustine's objections to his Old Testament translations. 'You must pardon my saying that you seem to me not to understand the matter.' In spite of his ignorance of the Hebrew language, Augustine had for many years been expounding the Psalms in a series of sermons. Numbers of these came into the hands of Jerome, who had no difficulty in pointing out some of his errors.

When someone from Hippo turned up in Bethlehem a year later, Jerome was disappointed to find he had never told Augustine he was coming, so brought no letter from him, but he seized the chance to send a note back by him to soften the impact of his own retort. 'That letter was not an answer from me to you, but a confrontation of my arguments with yours. If it was a fault in me to send a reply – I beseech you, hear me patiently – the fault of him who insisted upon it was greater. But let us be done with such quarrelling. Let there be sincere brotherly love between us. Let us henceforth exchange letters not of controversy but of mutual charity. Let us exercise ourselves in the field of Scripture without wounding each other.'

This was a fine gesture, though unfortunately Augustine took offence at the word Jerome had used for 'exercise ourselves', literally 'let us amuse ourselves'. So he returned to the attack, stoutly defending his opinion that 'at the time when the faith was first revealed' it was permissible for Paul and others to continue observing some of the ceremonies of the Mosaic Law. 'These observances were to be given up by all Christians, step by step, but not all at once. It never was my opinion that in our time Jews who become Christians are at liberty to observe the ceremonies of the ancient dispensation.'

Though in the main he gave no ground, he did admit that 'in many things Augustine is inferior to Jerome' and he at last agreed that it was beneficial for Jerome to translate direct from the original Hebrew. For several years they did not correspond, but Augustine could never get the old man out of his mind. 'My desire would be to have you daily beside me, as one with whom I could converse on any theme.' So he wrote him a long letter about Christianity and children, laying it down as beyond question that 'there is not one soul in the human family to whose salvation the one Mediator between God and men, the man Christ Jesus, is not absolutely necessary.' But in spite of all his 'praying, reading, thinking and reasoning', he was still not sure how to answer questions arising out of this conviction.

Where had the soul of a newborn infant contracted the guilt from which it could only be rescued by 'the grace of the Mediator and the sacrament of that grace', baptism? 'Where is the justice of the condemnation of so many thousands of souls which, in the death of infant children, leave the world without the benefit of the Christian sacrament?'

He found even greater difficulty in accounting for the pain, deformity and imbecility with which he saw some children afflicted. 'Now God is good, God is just, God is omnipotent: let the great suffering which infants experience be accounted for by some reason compatible with justice.' He frankly confessed to Jerome his need for help in these matters. 'I cannot think that it is at any time in life too late to learn what we need to know. I am embarrassed, believe me, by great difficulties and am wholly at a loss to find an answer.' He could not bring himself to evade 'the really difficult question', how a righteous God could justly condemn to eternal death innumerable innocent, unbaptized infants. 'If you have either read, or received from the Lord when meditating on this difficult question anything by which it can be solved, impart it to me, I beseech you.'

He did not get the reply for which he was hoping. Jerome, by this time in his mid-eighties, merely said that Augustine had already stated 'whatever can be drawn by commanding genius from the sacred Scriptures' on the subject.

12

Petilian: The Persecuted Believer

'Petilian, to his well-beloved brethren, fellow-priests and deacons, appointed ministers with us throughout our diocese in the gospel, grace be to you and peace, from God our Father and from the Lord Jesus Christ.' So began a letter from the Donatist bishop of Cirta (Constantine) to his colleagues, in which he spoke out strongly against the Catholic Church and Augustine in particular. Someone copied it for Augustine and he was urged at all costs to answer every point Petilian made. He explained, 'I will set down the words of his letter under his name and I will give the answer under my own name, as though it had all been taken down by reporters while we were debating.'

Petilian was a very different adversary from Faustus. He lacked both the learning and the eloquence of the Manichean. But he articulated the simple, biblical faith of the Berber Donatists and gave vent to the indignation of the mountain Christians at the bitter hostility shown to them by the Catholic Church, of which Augustine was the outstanding spokesman. Intellectually he was really no match for Augustine. He did not so much set out reasoned arguments as shout his defiance and then fall back upon lengthy quotations from the Bible. At the outset he made clear his opinion of the distinguished bishop of Hippo. 'You wicked persecutor, under whatever name of peace you wage war with kisses, you are the true son of the devil, showing your parentage by your character. You falsely call yourself a bishop. To you the Lord Christ will say, "Depart from me, you cursed, into everlasting fire."'

Too often in succeeding centuries the Donatist Church has been condemned on the testimony of Augustine. It is only right that we should listen for a while to what a Donatist leader thought of him. Petilian considered Augustine to be a murderer. 'Reckon up all the deaths of the saints – so often have you murdered Christ who lives in each of them. You, who call yourself a Christian, you do err, you do err, for God does not have butchers for His priests.' He quoted the whole of Psalm 1 against Augustine, then the whole of Psalm 23, then each of the Beatitudes from the Sermon on the Mount. 'On account of your wickedness the Lord does not know you. Your bloodstained conscience makes your prayers of no effect.'

Augustine defended himself with equal determination, denying everything Petilian had said, pouring scorn on him and his Church, claiming that the Donatists were themselves guilty of the very crimes they attributed to Catholics and pointing repeatedly to the harshness with which they had treated splinter groups of their own. So there was no meeting of minds, no mutual sympathy, only stark confrontation as he replied at some length to the brief statements he selected from his adversary's letter.

Petilian insisted that the Donatist Church did not feel free to retaliate. 'You carry on war without licence, but we may not fight in return. Our victory is either to escape or to be slain. To us the Lord has commanded simple patience and harmlessness.' Indignantly he demanded, 'What is the justification for persecution? Jesus Christ never persecuted anyone. On what principle do you persecute?' When Augustine referred to Christian love and equated it with ecclesiastical unity, he struck back at once. 'Love does not persecute. Love does not inflame emperors to take away the lives of other men, does not plunder other men's goods, does not go on to murder those whom it has spoiled. Where is your Christianity if you order such things to be done? You do not cease to murder us, who are just and poor – poor, that is in worldly wealth, for in the grace of God not one of us is poor. For even if you do not murder a man with your hands, you do not cease to do so with your butcherous tongues. All who have been murdered, you, the instigator of the deed, have slain. Nor does the hand of the butcher glow save at the instigation of your tongue. What Cain the murderer did once, you have often done, in slaying your brethren.'

For more than ten years Petilian maintained his defiance, suggesting that Augustine was still at heart a Manichean and blaming him for introducing monasticism to Africa, and for not allowing other men to be Christians in their own way but promoting unity by violence and war. To this Augustine answered, 'We don't kill you, but you kill yourselves when you cut yourselves off' (*Answer 2:23:52*). And he repelled the accusation of murder by an argument which enabled him to identify Donatism with spiritual murder. He stated that whoever separates from the only true Church is 'unable to defend himself from the charge of murder which is involved in the mere offence of dissension and schism, as the Scripture says, "Anyone who hates his brother is a murderer" (I John 3:15).' He justified the actions of the Catholic Church by reminding his opponent that Paul once delivered a man over to Satan for the destruction of his flesh so that his spirit might ultimately be saved. Referring to the expulsion of merchants from the temple with a whip (John 2:13-16), he deduced 'we do find Christ a persecutor'.

Claiming that it is right to take a sharp knife away from a child or to tie up a madman, he laid down the principle that 'it is better with severity to love than with gentleness to deceive'. So he unashamedly explained the change that had taken place in his own thinking. 'Originally my opinion was that no one should be coerced into the unity of Christ, that we must act only by words and fight only by arguments, prevailing by force of reason. But this opinion of mine was overcome, not by the words of those who controverted it, but by the conclusive instances to which they could point. In the first place my own town, though it was once wholly on the side of Donatus, was brought over to the Catholic unity by fear of the imperial edicts.'

There were plenty of others who told him how glad they were that strong measures had cured them of their Donatist blindness. So he persuaded himself that to shock and alarm people by 'the force of fear', to repress them by 'terrors of a temporal kind', to punish them by fines, confiscation and exile, and to deny them freedom in their business transactions and wills, was all a valid expression of Christian love since it rescued them from the crime of schism. Henceforth he regarded it as right to employ 'the formidable power of the authorities of this world' to assist the Church by bringing back into the fold those whom family tradition, apathy, slander, or the notion that 'it did not matter in what communion we hold the faith of Christ', kept among the Donatists.

In Christ's parable of the Great Supper in Luke 14 he found a New Testament parallel. At the beginning of the parable the servant is instructed to invite the guests, saying, 'Come, for everything is now ready.' This Augustine equated with the witness of the Church during the era of the pagan emperors prior to Constantine. Later in the parable the servant is sent out again and told to 'compel people to come in'. This he connected with the more favourable situation since the rulers of the Empire had professed the faith. Thus Augustine claimed the authority of Christ Himself for compelling others to enter the Catholic Church.

But he could not shake off a certain uneasiness. The memory of Cassiciacum, the mirage of the perfect tranquillity of Christian retirement, still beckoned him. He longed to escape from the harsh arena of public affairs. He frequently quoted Job 7:1, which in his version read, 'Is not the life of man upon earth a life of temptation?' He hoped an old friend of his in Rome might fall in with 'some judicious spiritual physician' who could advise him further on how Christians ought to live amongst men. 'If anything has become known to you through experience or meditation, or if you have already found or can learn anything from other teachers, I beseech you to give me instruction. I am most eagerly longing to be instructed by you.' And beyond all that he wished for heaven 'where the evils which we experience here shall have no place'.

13

A Time to Refrain from Embracing

From the opening of the fifth century danger signals had been flashing in the Roman sky. A vast migration of Goths, Huns, Vandals and other tribes was taking place and on 31 December 406, a mass crossing of the frozen Rhine near Mainz could not be prevented. The great city of Trier was destroyed and the invaders overran France, reaching the British Channel in the north, the Mediterranean Sea in the south and the Atlantic Ocean in the west. The legions stationed in Britain had to be withdrawn to defend the homeland.

Then Stilicho, himself a Vandal, fell under suspicion of being in league with the enemy and was executed at Ravenna, which henceforth became the residence of the Emperor Honorius in preference to both Rome and Milan. Hordes of desperate warriors were spreading fire and slaughter throughout western Europe. The scale of these events began to raise new intellectual problems for those who had time to think. Why were the servants of God cut off just as much as wicked men? Why were Christian women subjected to rape? Why should these awful things be happening to society at a time when Christianity was triumphant throughout the Empire? Had not conditions been more secure in the old days when the pagan gods were worshipped and the temples were full?

Early in 410 Augustine heard from a Greek-speaking student of rhetoric at Carthage named Dioscorus, who wanted immediate answers to a string of questions about the Dialogues of Cicero. Knowing of Augustine's former eminence in classical studies he boldly sent a messenger with several pages of questions.

At first Augustine was not at all pleased. 'When I consider how a bishop is distracted by the cares of his office clamouring on every side, it does not seem to me proper for him suddenly to withdraw from all these and devote himself to expounding to a single student some unimportant questions in the Dialogues of Cicero.' He was amazed that anyone should write from a cultural centre like Carthage to enquire on such a subject at Hippo, where he did not even know how to lay hands on manuscripts of Cicero's works. In his indignation he revealed that his hair was going white. But although he protested at the large number of questions the boy had asked, they awakened such memories that he dictated a thirty-page reply. He was able to do this because he was ill when the messenger arrived and during his convalescence away from Hippo he was unusually free to give his mind to such matters. He had never forgotten how much he owed to Cicero, whose learning and unique mastery of words he was still able to admire.

He also took the opportunity to tell Dioscorus that 'in our day no error dares to rally round it the uninstructed crowd without seeking the shelter of the Christian name'. In his experience the older Greek teachers posed no great threat to the gospel message. He felt that Plato had come much nearer to the truth than other philosophers and he knew many Christians who had great affection for him because of the charm of his style and the accuracy of many of his insights. 'With the intuition of genius he observed the invisible realities of God' to some extent, though still a long way from full understanding. Along with all this he pointed Dioscorus to Jesus Christ, the way and the truth. 'In that way the first part is humility. This I would continue to repeat as often as you might ask direction, not that there are no other instructions which may be given but because, unless humility precede, accompany and follow every good action which we perform, pride wrests wholly from our hand any good work on which we are congratulating ourselves. All other vices are to be apprehended when we are doing wrong, but pride is to be feared even when we do right.'

In his weakness he found it hard to endure the cold and the heavy rain which afflicted North Africa during the 'exceptionally dreadful winter' in the early months of 410. He had to stay away from Hippo so long that his congregation rather lost patience with him and suspended the custom of providing clothes for the poor which, under his influence, they had maintained for many years. He attributed it partly to moral sloth in reaction to the reports from Europe of calamities so shocking that they seemed to be the fulfilment of what Christ had predicted would precede the end of the world.

With the coming of kinder weather he recovered his strength and was back at his post by the day which signalled a momentous change in the history of the western world. On 24 August 410, Rome fell to the forces of Alaric the Goth. After eight hundred years of imperial supremacy, the eternal city was given up to several days of carnage, burning and looting by the victorious soldiers from eastern Europe. However, the Goths respected church buildings and spared the lives of many who sought sanctuary in them. Honorius remained powerless at Ravenna, secure behind the marshes near the mouth of the River Po.

Knowing that Rome's million inhabitants had been supplied with grain from Africa, Alaric planned to take his people over to Carthage, searching for a land where he could settle them in safety. His army moved down into the toe of Italy where, across a few miles of water, the mountains of Sicily loomed like a huge stepping stone bisecting the Mediterranean. Africa trembled at what was to come, but Alaric's transports were wrecked in a storm, the invasion plan had to be dropped and his army turned back from what had proved to be a cul-de-sac. That same autumn of 410 he died. His men diverted a river, buried him in its bed, brought the river back over his grave, and massacred all the prisoners who had done the work and knew where the great commander lay. Thus the Gothic battering ram lost its driving power. Meanwhile the Atlantic wing of the barbarian invasion surged over the Pyrenees and spread havoc through Spain. The Vandals, who had started from their base in Hungary, eventually settled in the mountains behind Gibraltar where the region of Andalusia still suggests their name.

Africa was not invaded by the Goths but by wealthy Roman refugees. Quite a sensation was created in Carthage by the arrival of a family headed by a widow named Proba whose sons had held high office in Rome. Having survived the fall of the city and then escaped from Italy while Alaric's army was in the south of the country, she reached Africa safely along with her daughter-in-law Juliana, also widowed, and Juliana's daughter Demetrias. Many other widows and girls travelled with these refined ladies. On reaching Carthage Proba was compelled to part with a considerable percentage of her fortune in favour of the Count of Africa, before he would allow her company to settle in the city.

In due course Proba wrote to Augustine, asking his advice about prayer. An exchange of letters followed and on his frequent visits to Carthage the ladies heard him preach. As a result, although arrangements for the marriage of Demetrias had already been completed, she decided to take a vow of chastity and become a nun. Augustine and Alypius wrote her a joint letter to express their satisfaction and give her their advice.

Ever since his conversion Augustine had held aloof from personal relationships with women. None were allowed to enter the monastery where he lived, not even his own widowed sister or the daughters of his brother Navigius. In spite of this rigorous segregation and the sad experiences of his youth, Augustine's work as pastor and magistrate had given him wide knowledge of other people's struggles. Thus equipped, he wrote a series of books on marriage, celibacy and widowhood, expounding the biblical statements on such matters but also reflecting the strong prejudice of the age in favour of celibacy.

In one sense Augustine had a very high estimate of marriage. 'God instituted marriage from the beginning, before man's fall.' He approved marriage for life to one person only and was opposed to fornication before marriage, to adultery after it, and to divorce. Death alone terminated marriage, so that if a couple separated 'they continue wedded persons even after separation' and would be guilty of adultery if either remarried. On the death of a partner he allowed remarriage, refusing to condemn even a third or fourth marriage after bereavements. But this acknowledgement of the validity of the married state was modified by his insistence that sexual intercourse between husband and wife should be limited to what was absolutely necessary for the birth of children. In that he saw no fault, but he considered any further physical relations essentially faulty, requiring God's pardon, for they 'no longer followed reason, but lust', though he was prepared to grant that some good came out of the evil because people were thereby restrained from the deadly sin of adultery. This conviction was not weakened by his confession that in conversation with Christian couples he had never found any who had succeeded in limiting their relationship in this way.

In another sense Augustine had a low estimate of marriage

because he so emphatically preferred celibacy. 'The weaker brothers in the married state, who have children or hope to have them' he contrasted with 'those who have a higher standard of life, who are not entangled with the bonds of matrimony'. When interpreting Christ's parable of the sower he inclined to identify those who bore fruit thirty-fold with married Christians, those who bore fruit sixty-fold with widows who refrained from marrying again, and those who bore fruit a hundred-fold with the celibate, 'virgins, holy boys and girls, trained up in the Church'. Times without number he reiterated that while marriage is good, to avoid it is better, much better. 'The virginity of your child', he assured Juliana, 'has compensated for the loss of your virginity. Coming after you in birth, she has risen above you in honour and gone before you in holiness.' He anticipated that in heaven there would be special rewards for the virgins of Christ, such as would not be experienced by the rest of the faithful. 'The others are below in work and wages.' He never ceased to advocate, in preference to matrimony, the holier spiritual marriage to Christ, 'the Spouse of virgins'.

He returned again and again to the defence of the polygamy of the Jewish patriarchs, arming himself with the verse which says there is 'a time to embrace and a time to refrain from embracing' (Ecclesiastes 3:5). With passionate oratory he explained that the Old Testament era was the time to embrace, for it was essential that the people of God should multiply as a preparation for the gospel and that prophets of Christ's coming might arise among them. Indeed he suggested that the whole Jewish race was then 'nothing else but a Prophet of Christ' and that for this reason righteous men were allowed more than one wife, not because they were overcome by lust but because they were 'led by piety'. He insisted that the patriarchs had physical relations with their wives solely for the purpose of having children. 'They felt no unlawful lust for any of them.' Such married life he held to be prophetic, God's deep plan lying hidden in it, so that it was a matter of obedience to God. He looked forward to sitting down with all true believers in the kingdom of heaven along with Abraham, Isaac and Jacob who 'for the sake of Christ were husbands, for the sake of Christ were fathers'.

In contrast, Augustine viewed the age in which he himself lived as the time to refrain from embracing. The people of God had become numerous in many nations. There was no further need to serve Christ's coming by having children. Now that He had come, He was better served by restraint. No duty to mankind required marriage to be undertaken. Only those who could not otherwise control themselves should embark upon it, for it had become no more than a remedy for human weakness.

So he did his best to discourage Juliana from contemplating a second marriage. He presumed she would not descend to the use of make-up, and he warned her and Demetrias not to become proud of their abstinence and to beware lest the desire for money replaced the desire for marriage. He regretted that he had known many virgins who had become talkative, drunken, covetous and proud, so he counselled his readers against wandering eyes, unbridled tongues, petulant laughs, scurrilous jests, against 'bosses of hair swelling out and coverings so yielding that the fine network below appears'. Believing obedience to be the mother of all virtues, he went so far as to state that 'a more obedient married woman is to be preferred to a less obedient virgin'. But, having said that, he advised the ladies to turn their backs on the delights of matrimony and to devote themselves instead to reading and prayer, to singing psalms and meditating on the law of God, to frequent good works and hopes of the world to come, to gazing on the beauty of Christ, remembering His blood and the price He paid for their redemption. 'Whatever love you had to expend upon your marriages, pay back to Him.'

In view of these convictions it is not surprising that Augustine had a profound respect for the Virgin Mary, but instead of adhering to the facts recorded in the Gospels he accepted some superstitious beliefs about her which were already current. 'Before she knew who was to be born of her,' he maintained, 'she had already vowed herself to God as a virgin. Having conceived without being touched by man, she always remained thus untouched, in virginity conceiving, in virginity bringing forth, in virginity dying. Joseph had no carnal knowledge of her. There had never been, nor was there ever meant to be, any carnal connection. There was fidelity but no mutual cohabitation. They never even began to cohabit' (*Virginity 4, Instruction 22:40, Marriage 1:12-13*).

These assertions led inevitably to a further assumption. 'The blood relations of the Virgin Mary used to be called the Lord's brothers, for it was the usage of Scripture to call near kindred by the term "brothers". Abraham and Lot are called brothers, though Abraham was Lot's uncle. So, when you hear of the Lord's brothers, consider them the blood relations of Mary, who did not bear children a second time' (*Tractate 28:3*).

Moreover, though Augustine agreed that 'If we say we have no sin, we deceive ourselves', he felt that 'We must except the Virgin Mary, concerning whom I wish to raise no question on the subject of sins, out of honour to the Lord, for we know from Him what abundance of grace for overcoming sin in every particular was conferred on her who had the merit to conceive and bear Him who undoubtedly had no sin' (*Nature 42*).

14

Love and Do What You Like

Soon after Rome had fallen to the Goths, the Emperor Honorius, still secure at Ravenna, sent to Africa a special representative named Marcellinus, charged with the task of putting an end to the Donatist problem. In June 4II he summoned both parties to a conference at Carthage which was attended by no fewer than 570 bishops, 286 of them Catholic and 284 Donatist. It was not really a conference at all but a grim confrontation in order to pronounce formal condemnation on the Donatists, who found they had become an illegal, criminal organisation. Unless they agreed to become Catholic as entire communities, their church buildings had to be surrendered. Their bishops and clergy were fined and all Donatist property was, 'through the religious laws of our Christian emperors' as Augustine put it, confiscated and given to the Catholic Church. In succeeding years those who remained obstinate lost all civil rights, were turned out of the towns in which they lived, and in some cases deported to remote parts of the sprawling Empire.

Thanks to such violent measures, the challenge of the Donatist Church to ecclesiastical unity ceased to be significant. When all allowance has been made for the Emperor's anxiety to achieve a united Africa at a time of war, it has to be admitted that Augustine lent his great authority to cruel proceedings, carried out in the name of Christian love, which set a disastrous precedent for subsequent generations. The strength of Christianity among the African peasants and intellectuals lay in the Donatist Church. It can be argued that by invoking the power of the state to eradicate Donatism by legal, financial and military pressures Augustine did more damage to the worldwide cause of the Christian Church than all the benefits conferred upon it by the genius of his personality and teaching.

Marcellinus and Augustine were drawn closely together by the struggle in which they had played such significant roles. In Carthage Marcellinus was in touch with a circle of cultured Romans who used to meet in the evenings for friendly discussion. On some occasion when the group had been discussing poetry and philosophy for a long time, one of the company boldly confessed he had grave doubts about the truth of Christianity and found the virgin birth of Christ incredible. He questioned very much whether the ruler of the whole world could possibly have become an insignificant infant and suggested the miracles recorded in the Gospels could be paralleled elsewhere and were in any case 'but small works for God to do'. At this the others prevented him from saying anything more and the meeting broke up. Then they wrote to ask Augustine for his help. 'Ignorance may, without harm to religion, be tolerated in other priests, but when we come to Bishop Augustine, whatever we find unknown to him is no part of the Christian system.' As was his custom, Augustine rejected any suggestion that he was infallible. 'Such is the depth of the Christian Scriptures', he replied, 'that even if I were attempting to study them and nothing else from early boyhood to decrepit old age with the utmost leisure, the most unwearied zeal, and talents greater than I have, I would still be daily making progress in discovering their treasures.' Busy as he was with all the work involved in the leadership of his community, in preaching and counselling as well as writing several books simultaneously, he still managed to find time for an extended reply, postponing other matters which he had intended dictating to his secretaries.

Meanwhile Marcellinus confided in Augustine that the group was troubled by many other problems about Christianity. They were perplexed because the God of the New Testament was said to have abrogated what He had commanded in the Old Testament, thus laying Himself open to the charge of inconsistency. Furthermore, they felt that Christian teaching was incompatible with the duties of Roman citizens, especially because it advocated turning the other cheek and not recompensing evil for evil, precepts which could hardly be applied at a time when the Empire was being attacked by barbarian invaders. Then there was the worrying fact that such great disasters should have occurred when the emperors professed to be Christians.

Augustine sent his reply to Marcellinus alone, leaving it to him to use his discretion in sharing it with the others. With regard to the change from 'the comparative darkness of the Old Testament', he asked, 'Does not summer follow winter, the temperature gradually increasing in warmth? How often our own lives experience changes. Boyhood departing, never to return, gives place to youth; manhood, destined itself to continue only for a season, takes in turn the place of youth; and old age, closing the term of manhood, is itself closed by death. All these things are changed, but the plan of divine providence which appoints these successive changes is not changed.'

He suggested that the commands in the Sermon on the Mount ought not to be taken too literally, since neither Christ nor Paul actually turned the other cheek when struck, but rather protested, suggesting that such verses relate to a Christian's attitude, not to his precise actions. Then he appealed directly to the group. 'Let those who say that the doctrine of Christ is incompatible with the state's wellbeing give us an army composed of soldiers such as the doctrine of Christ requires them to be: let them give us such subjects, such husbands and wives, such parents and children, such masters and servants, such kings, such judges, such taxpayers and tax gatherers as the Christian religion has taught that men should be, and then let them dare to say that it is adverse to the state's wellbeing. Rather, let them confess that this doctrine, if it were obeyed, would be the salvation of the commonwealth.'

He had no difficulty in quoting from the historian Sallust and the poet Juvenal to prove that the downfall of the Romans began long before there were any Christian emperors and that in past centuries prosperity led to unlimited wickedness, when 'dire corruption, more terrible than any invader, took possession of the mind of the state'. In such circumstances he unashamedly regarded the cross of Christ as a wonderful deliverance from the vile abyss of depravity into which men were helplessly sinking.

Some years earlier Augustine had embarked upon an ambitious series of 124 sermons in which he expounded the Gospel of John section by section. At Easter 415 he interrupted this to explain the First Epistle of John in ten sermons delivered in the course of only eight days. Though he did not use a single story in illustration, he so held the attention of his audience day by day that at times they cried out in approval or were stirred to applause.

'I ask you today for your closest attention, since we have no light matter to consider,' he said as he came to I John 3:9. 'Indeed the interest with which you listened to yesterday's sermon assures me that it will be even keener today. For the question to be raised is a very difficult one. We are asking what is meant by this text in our Epistle, "No one who is born of

God will continue to sin" in view of that earlier saying in the same Epistle, "If we claim to be without sin, we deceive ourselves and the truth is not in us." Now give your minds to these words. I want you to face the difficulty.'

With such an Epistle in front of him, Augustine laid his Easter emphasis upon God's love to us and the love to others which it demands from us. 'The words are not mine', he declared. 'If it were I that said "God is love" any of you might take offence and say "What was that? What did he mean?" There, my brethren, is God's Scripture before you: this is a canonical epistle, read in every nation. Here you are told by the Spirit of God, "God is love" (I John 4:8). Now, if you dare, act against God and refuse to love your brother.'

He insisted that 'love is the only final distinction between the sons of God and the sons of the devil'. He roundly declared that anyone could be baptized, attend church, cross himself, receive the sacrament, answer Amen, sing Hallelujah, or utter prophecies, but love alone distinguished the true Christian from others, love alone was the special gift of the Spirit. 'At the church's beginning the Holy Spirit fell upon the believers and they spoke with tongues unlearnt', he reminded them. 'It was a sign fitted to the time: all the world's tongues were a fitting signification of the Holy Spirit, because the gospel of God was to have its course through every tongue in all parts of the earth. The sign was given and then passed away. We no longer expect that those upon whom the hand is laid that they may receive the Holy Spirit will speak with tongues. When we laid our hand upon these "infants", the Church's newborn members, none of you (I think) looked to see if they would speak with tongues or, seeing that they did not, had the perversity to argue that they had not received the Holy Spirit. If then the Holy Spirit's presence is no longer testified by such marvels, on what is anyone to ground his assurance that he has received the Holy Spirit? Let him enquire of his own heart: if he loves his brother, the Spirit of God abides in him.'

'A short and simple precept is given you once for all', he said in the seventh of these Easter talks, when he was explaining the definitive statement about the love of God in I John 4:9. 'Love and do what you like. Whether you keep silence, keep silence in love; whether you exclaim, exclaim in love; whether you correct, correct in love; whether you forbear, forbear in love. Let love's root be within you and from that root nothing but good can spring. Who can do ill to any person whom he loves? Love, and you cannot but do well.' Torn from their context, his memorable words 'Love and do what you like' have sometimes been used to justify immoral behaviour so long as it is accompanied by feelings of intense affection. Indeed, the idea misled Augustine himself. Identifying love with unity in subjection to the Catholic Church, he felt no Christian obligation to show what would normally be recognized as kindness, gentleness or friendliness towards those outside the only Church he acknowledged.

******

Around the year 420 the last known episode in the long struggle to liquidate the Donatist Church took place. An official named Dulcitius was sent from Italy to demand the submission of the Donatists at Timgad, near the Aures Mountains, where the great Donatist cathedral still maintained its independence under Gaudentius, its defiant bishop. Eyeing the well-armed imperial forces closing in on them, Gaudentius and his people determined to deny the Romans the chance of deciding their fate. The church was turned into a fortress and he informed

Dulcitius that they would burn it down over their own heads if they were attacked.

The confrontation lasted several months. Gaudentius reminded the officer he was facing, and Augustine who was the driving force behind him, that 'the Saviour of souls, the Lord Christ, sent fishermen, not soldiers, to make the faith known'. He denied that God, the judge of the living and the dead, looked for the help of a worldly army. He suggested they might like to remember the words of Christ Himself about the good shepherd who laid down His life for the sheep and the wolf who 'attacks the flock and scatters it'. He could see no 'safe and peaceful harbour' for himself and other leaders 'tossed from every quarter in this stormy persecution'. He felt they were in a worse position than the original apostles whom the Lord told to flee from one town to another, because in those days people who sheltered them were not liable to severe punishment.

Augustine saw it all quite differently. 'They cannot have the death of martyrs', he declared, 'because they do not have the life of Christians.' He had met this threat to commit suicide before, 'the mad aberration of a few men', and he was not going to be moved by it. 'It is better for some of them to perish in their own fire, than that all should equally burn in the eternal fires of hell as a punishment for their accursed dissension.'

We do not know what happened. The massive triumphal archway, standing guard over the paved roads and ruined houses of Timgad to this day, tells no tales.

15

Pelagius: Champion of Free Will

Meanwhile a humble but historically important refugee had reached the coast of Africa. Pelagius, a layman some years younger than Augustine, a gifted teacher of the Christian faith, came originally from Britain. He had lived for many years in Rome, where he wrote books on some New Testament Epistles and Christian morality. He came to feel that the emphasis laid by the Church on the doctrine of original sin, on the weakness of human nature, and on the absolute necessity for the grace of God, encouraged moral inertia by making people think they neither could nor need do anything themselves, being mere puppets in the hands of their Creator.

'I first became acquainted with Pelagius' name, along with great praise of him', recorded Augustine, 'when he was living in Rome, but afterwards reports reached us that he disputed against the grace of God. In the last few days I have read some of his writings. I am told he is a holy man who has made no small progress in the Christian life. On his arrival in Africa he was in my absence kindly received on our coast of Hippo.' However, Pelagius did not stay long. Later on, in Carthage, 'I caught a glimpse of him, once or twice to the best of my recollection, when I was very much occupied preparing for a conference we were to hold with the Donatists.' This was the only occasion they met and by the time Augustine was free to pay attention to him, Pelagius had left for Jerusalem, never to return to Africa. 'Meanwhile the doctrines connected with his name were warmly maintained and passed from mouth to mouth among his reputed followers.'

So far was Pelagius from nourishing any personal ill will towards Augustine that he wrote to him cordially. Now that the chance had gone Augustine found himself 'greatly longing to have a conversation with him in person', so he replied briefly. 'I thank you very much for your letter. May the Lord requite you with His blessing, my beloved and longed for brother. Pray for me.' With Pelagius calling on Jerome in Bethlehem, the issues he had raised began to attract attention around the Christianised Roman world.

Although he had no wish to oppose the Catholic Church or question the authority of the Bible, Pelagius' teaching did constitute a reconsideration of accepted views about the fall of man and the doctrine of original sin transmitted from Adam to the entire human race. 'Adam's sin injured only Adam himself' epitomized this attitude. In his study of the New Testament Pelagius had been struck by the emphasis laid on the force of example, the example of Christ, and the example of Paul. He maintained we are all born in a morally neutral state, without virtue and without vice. Adam sinned by his own choice. His descendants sin in the same way, following his bad example. Sin, he insisted, 'is not born with us but done by us'. He could not tolerate the idea that God, who forgives sin, actually imputes Adam's sin to us when we are in a state of uncomprehending innocence.

Human beings at birth he regarded as in the same condition as Adam before he disobeyed God, free to choose good or evil. He insisted that the fall of Adam has no more automatic effect on others than does the resurrection of Christ: what Christ did is only effective for the man who makes it his own by faith; what Adam did is only damaging for the man who makes it his own by imitation. This led Pelagius to deny that original sin was a punishable offence. He felt it was monstrous to suggest that infants who died unbaptized would perish. Like Jerome, he believed that each soul was newly created by God, not derived from parents along with the body, so he did not regard sin as an inherited infection but as something each individual either did or did not choose to do. Thus, though he was as aware as Augustine of the wickedness of contemporary society, he denied that this depravity was transmitted from the first man or that infants were damned, unless in due course they themselves chose to do evil.

None of this meant that Pelagius was a humanist who turned his back on the revelation of God in the Bible or that he was obsessed with the ability of man to improve himself. He remained an ardent Christian, seeking to understand and apply all aspects of New Testament teaching, believing that 'the grace of God, whereby Christ Jesus came into the world to save sinners, is necessary not only for every hour and every moment but also for every act of our lives'. However, he used the word in an inclusive sense. To him God's grace embraced His endowment of mankind with free will, the forgiveness of sins through the death of Christ, the example of Christ and the teaching of Christ. Such views inclined him to employ allegory sparingly, to make more use of the New Testament than the Old, and to underline the moral aspects of Christ's teaching recorded in the Gospels as a corrective to the contemporary tendency to exalt doctrinal orthodoxy above everything else. He wanted to maintain the reasonable balance he found in the New Testament between God's work and man's response. Convinced that the capacity for right thinking, speaking and acting is God's gift to mankind, he was equally convinced that it is we ourselves who actually choose to think, speak and act righteously. Although he founded no separate church, what came to be called Pelagianism was soon in evidence all over the Roman Empire. 'Let us ponder these things day and night, my friends', he said. 'It is a great thing to be a son of God, to possess eternal life in all its richness and to have the prospect of the joys of reigning with God in heaven. Let us then strive with all the powers at our command to overcome sin and dip ourselves deep in activities of holiness and righteousness, that we may not undergo the sufferings of the damned but enjoy the blessed state together with the righteous.'

Emphasising in this way the part played by man's free will, Pelagius found himself in diametrical opposition to the idea that by God's inscrutable decree a limited number were chosen for salvation while the majority of mankind were condemned to be lost. In his opinion this made nonsense of God's clearly expressed desire that all men should be saved. Such a text as Romans 9:18, 'God has mercy on whom He wants to have mercy, and He hardens whom He wants to harden', was particularly difficult for him to accept. He decided the statement must be a gloss inserted by an opponent of the gospel, for he was convinced it was only the devil who hardened men's hearts. Struggling to interpret the Scriptures correctly, while avoiding outrageous assertions about God, he came to identify predestination with foreknowledge. He taught that God does not will the damnation of anyone: men condemn themselves by rejecting God's love; predestination is simply that God foreknows this, knows it before it happens; it is only a chronological accident that His foreknowledge precedes the event, for it does not determine it, but rather vice versa. The strongest evidence for the effectiveness of his appeal was that before long Augustine embarked upon a tremendous series of books and booklets designed to refute the arguments of the layman from Britain. The more he studied Pelagius' books the more his opinion hardened that this emphasis constituted 'a poisonous perversion of the truth'. He sharply distinguished the issues Pelagius had raised from secondary matters on which divergent views were permissible. Eventually he abandoned all restraint and openly attacked him as an enemy of the grace of God.

Speaking of original sin, the most fundamental issue involved in the debate, he reiterated that 'all of us are born in sin: our very origin is sin', the only exception being Christ the Mediator, born of a virgin without the intervention of human desire. Though regretting that conception is 'impracticable without a certain amount of bestial motion which puts human nature to the blush', he did not blame marriage for the transmission of original sin but only human desire, which he never failed to call 'lust'. As a result he maintained that infants, though incapable of sinning, 'are not born without the contagion of sin, not because of what is lawful (marriage) but on account of what is unseemly (lust)'. He argued that this universal birth stain could only be purged by baptism, the bath of regeneration, for nothing but the second birth could deliver from the bondage inherent in the first birth.

He regarded Adam's disobedience recorded in the third chapter of Genesis as 'a misuse of free will which started a chain of disaster, for we were all in that one man, seeing that we all were that one man'. Struggling to understand what it was that caused Adam to make the original wrong choice, since God had created him without sin, he came to the conclusion that this was 'like trying to see darkness or hear silence, so no one must try to get to know from me what I know that I do not know'. In asserting that men are born perverted, not morally neutral, he claimed to have the support of history and experience as well as Scripture. 'What else is the message of all the evils of humanity?'

Pelagius' views about predestination forced Augustine to review his own convictions, but not to change them. 'When questions of this sort come before us, why this one is blinded by being forsaken by God and that one enlightened by divine aid, let us not take upon ourselves to pass judgment on the judgment of so mighty a judge.' Although occasionally admitting that 'this is too high for my stature and too strong for my strength,' he was not prepared to make any concessions to human sentiment. 'A deserved penalty is meted out to the damned, an undeserved grace to the saved; the former cannot complain that he is undeserving nor the latter boast that he is deserving.'

Augustine insisted that grace precedes faith, that Christians choose God because they have been chosen by Him, that God does whatever He wills to do, 'to bestow kindness on some and to heap punishment on others, as He Himself judges right', but this caused great distress to many people whose reaction was to say that if everything depended on God then they themselves should not be rebuked for anything they did. 'Why is it my fault', they asked, 'if I don't have what I have not received from Him, when He alone can give it?'

In response to this, Augustine asserted that the number of the predestined was fixed before the world began, 'neither to be increased nor diminished', but added that no one could be sure he was one of the elect so long as he was alive, since it was always possible that he had not been granted the gift of perseverance. 'To some of His own children whom He has regenerated in Christ, to whom He has given faith, hope and love, God does not give perseverance also.' Failure to persevere would prove that, after all, the person was not one of the elect.

When confronted with Paul's statement that God 'wants all men to be saved' (I Tim. 2:4), he declared that by analogy with the use of the word in other New Testament passages 'all' meant 'all the predestined'. He denied that the verse could possibly mean that people are not saved simply because they are unwilling to believe. It is 'not because *they* do not will it but because God does not', for he regarded it as beyond question that God 'did not will to do anything that He has not done'.

A youth named Hilary wrote to Augustine explaining that many people in Marseilles were disturbed by 'this new theory' which seemed to make preaching useless. They could not accept the idea that the number of the elect had already been fixed, as to some extent the issue must depend on the use each man made of the free will God had given him. Augustine's words made people despair. Conscious of his immaturity and admitting that 'all of us are weary of it', Hilary arranged for a theologian named Prosper to write to Augustine too.

'Many of the servants of Christ who live in the city of Marseilles', explained Prosper, 'think that your argument on the calling of the elect according to the design of God is contrary to the opinion of the Fathers and the tradition of the Church.' The objectors asserted that 'the blood of Christ was offered for all men without exception, hence all who are willing to approach to faith and baptism can be saved'. To say that the question of personal salvation or damnation had already been settled 'according to the pleasure of the Creator' would undermine all effort, since 'the outcome cannot be other than what God has determined and under the name of predestination a certain inevitability of fate is introduced'. In their opinion, however, 'Our Lord Jesus Christ died for the whole human race: as far as God is concerned, eternal life is prepared for all; but as far as the freedom of the will is concerned, eternal life is won by those who believe by their own choice.'

Augustine replied to Hilary and Prosper in two books, *The Predestination of the Saints* and *The Gift of Perseverance*. To his critics he yielded not one inch. He admitted that earlier in life 'I was in a similar error, thinking that the faith whereby we believe in God is in us from ourselves and that by it we obtain the gifts of God', but he had been compelled to change his mind, mainly by Paul's words, 'What do you have that you did not receive?' (I Cor. 4:7). He therefore reaffirmed his conviction that 'grace precedes faith'. Only those whom God has predestined to be His children become believers. Tirelessly he drummed it into his readers that 'God elected believers: He chose them that they might be so, not because they already were so.' Men do not believe in order to be numbered with the elect: they are 'elected to believe'. And he flatly denied the Pelagian suggestion that God predestined Christians to be His children because He foresaw that they would believe.

The longer he went on the more inflexible he became. With his uncanny ability to draw Scripture verses to his aid, he confronted critics of God's fairness with the landowner's answers to his indignant employees in Christ's parable of the labourers in the vineyard, 'Take what belongs to you, and go. I choose to give to this last as I give to you. Am I not allowed to do what I choose with what belongs to me?' (Matt. 20:14-15.) Asked why one person should be punished by God and another delivered, he replied, 'I can find no answer; as His anger is righteous and His mercy great, so His judgments are unsearchable.'

He did not shirk the problem posed by Christ's admission that the inhabitants of Tyre and Sidon would have repented if they had witnessed the deeds He did in other places. 'Although he foresaw that they would believe His miracles if they should be done among them, He willed not to come to their help since in His predestination – secret indeed but yet righteous – He had determined otherwise concerning them.' It was just the same with unbaptized infants. 'Often when the parents are eager and the ministers prepared for giving baptism, it is still not given.' Why not? Because God had not elected those children before the foundation of the world to be Christians. So what happens to them? 'Not being regenerated, they pass into the second death and the wrath of God abides on them.' To those who were shocked at this conclusion his reply was, 'Again and again we say "Who are you, O man, to answer back to God?"' (Rom. 9:20.)

In thus leaving no loophole for compassion, Augustine claimed to be rightly interpreting the New Testament. 'Let those who think I am in error consider again and again what is said here, lest perchance they themselves may be mistaken.'

16

Free Will and God's Will

'Do not say, "The Lord is to blame for my failure".
It is for you to avoid doing what He hates.
When He made us in the beginning,
He left us free to take our own decisions.
If you choose, you can keep the commandments.
Whether or not you keep faith is yours to decide.'
(Ecclesiasticus 15:11, 14-15)

Late in life Augustine quoted this striking passage from the Apocrypha. 'Observe how very plainly the free choice of the human will is set before us. God has revealed to us through His Holy Scriptures that our will is free.' Then he cited twenty-eight of God's commands from both Testaments, all presupposing that we are free to obey them or not. 'Wherever it is said "do this" or "do not do that", there is at once a proof of free will' (*Grace 1-4*). From the start of his Christian life this had always been his conviction. 'Sin occurs through free will. Nothing makes a mind give way to desire except its own choice. God has not compelled us to sin just because He gave us the power to choose between sinning and not sinning' (*Choice 2:1:3* with *1:11:21, 3:5:14, 3:18:49*). So he professed himself a champion of free will. 'It is true that the soul has received free will. Those who try to discredit this by baseless arguments are blind. Yet the gift of free will is such that, no matter what the soul undertakes with it, it does not disturb any part of the divine order. It is a gift coming from the Lord of all creation' (*Greatness 36:80*).

He insisted that both the beginning and the satisfactory progress of the Christian life hinge upon our being willing. So when he came to expound 1 John 3:3, 'Everyone who has this hope in Christ purifies himself', he pointed out, 'See how he has not taken away free will, in that he says "purifies himself". It is only God who can purify you, yet God does not purify you if you are unwilling. You purify yourself in joining your will to God. You purify yourself not by yourself but by Him who dwells in you. Because your will shares in this, something is attributed to you. In asking for His help you are doing something' (*Homily 4:7*).

He was convinced that the greatest of all God's works was the creation of intelligent human beings. 'On these intellectual natures He bestowed the power of free choice which enabled them, if they so chose, to desert God, judging it a greater act to bring good out of evil than to exclude the existence of evil. He did not deprive them of the power of free choice. So, when you feel that you do not understand, put your faith in the inspired word of God and believe both that our will is free and that without God's help it cannot turn towards God. We could exercise no obedience without free will' (*City 22:1, Letter 214:7*). He could not agree with Cicero that to believe God knows future events is fatal to belief in free will. On the contrary, 'We assert both that God knows all things before they happen and that we do by our own free will everything that we know would not happen without our volition' (*City 5:9*).

Having established the fact that human beings are endowed by God with free will, Augustine laid down in the most uncompromising terms his opinion about the will of God Almighty. 'Nothing happens but by the will of the Omnipotent,

He either permitting it to be done or doing it Himself. God does well even in the permission of what is evil, for He permits it only in the justice of His judgment. The Omnipotent God can as easily refuse to permit what He does not wish, as to bring about what He does wish. If we do not believe this, the very first sentence of our creed, in which we assert that God is "the Father Almighty", is endangered. Even what is done in opposition to His will does not defeat His will, for it would not be done if He did not permit it, and of course His permission is not unwilling but willing. A Good Being would not permit evil to be done, except that in His omnipotence He can turn evil into good. However strong may be the purposes of men, whether these fall in with the will of God or run counter to it, the will of the Omnipotent is never defeated. He is never unjust in what He does, never does anything except by His own free will, and never wills anything that He does not perform' (*Enchiridion 95, 96, 100, 102*). On these principles Augustine insists that God alone chooses those who are to be saved: 'No one can trust in the help of God without God's help' (*City 14:27*). So the Christian Church is 'the predestined Church', consisting only of those whom God has 'predestined to salvation' and excluding those whom God has already 'predestined to go into the eternal fire with the devil' (*City 20:7* and *21:24*).

Some people found such statements alarming, but he was not disposed to modify them. 'There is no injustice in God not willing that they should be saved, though they could have been saved had He willed it. He is not truly called Almighty if He cannot do whatever He pleases or if the power of His almighty will is hindered by the will of any one He has created' (*Enchiridion 95, 96*). Although Christ, looking over Jerusalem, said, 'How often would I have gathered your children together as a hen gathers her brood under her wings, but you would not', he maintained it was wrong to understand this 'as if the will of God had been overcome by the will of men', preferring to assume that 'He gathered together as many as He wished, even though they were unwilling' (*Enchiridion 97*). But by such reasoning he evacuated the Lord's words of their plain meaning.

When people expressed dismay at hearing that God's will was the cause not only of 'the eternal happiness of the righteous' but also of 'the everlasting pains of the ungodly', he repeatedly appealed to Romans 11:33, 'How unsearchable are His judgments' and to Romans 9:20, 'Who are you, O man, to talk back to God?' He pointed out that physical strength, good health, beauty, intellectual capacity, and innumerable other qualities were 'given by the Lord to some and not to others' (*Rebuke 19*). Accused of lapsing into fatalism, he replied, 'They think that we assert fate under the name of grace, but it is rather they who call divine grace fate' (*Two Letters 2:10, 12*).

Since Christ said, 'You have not chosen me, but I have chosen you' and Paul 'God has chosen us in Him before the foundation of the world' he insisted that 'God elected believers. People do not believe in order to be elected. They are elected to believe. He chose them so that they might choose Him. This is the changeless truth concerning predestination. Yet undoubtedly they did choose Him when they believed on Him' (*Predestination 34*), and he drew upon an avalanche of biblical texts in support of his conviction that 'no one even begins to be changed from evil to good unless the mercy of God effects this. The faith by which we are Christians is the gift of God' (*Predestination 3*). In conformity with this, he maintained that the words of 2 Corinthians 4:4, 'the god of this world has blinded the minds of those who do not believe', far from referring to the devil, plainly signified that 'The true and just God blinds the minds of unbelievers' (*Faustus 21:2*).

By day Augustine was a local man, Hippo's most famous citizen, the friend and guide of its people, arbitrator in disputes, fascinating teacher of Christian truth. He knew the struggles and failures of their lives, so that he could speak straight into their hearts – and they loved it. But by night he was an international man, secluded with a group of scribes, addressing readers all round the Mediterranean, a vast invisible congregation whose struggles were hidden from him. Many of them were hanging on his words too, but in this context he spoke a little less personally, though always with the Bible open.

To the familiar faces so close to him he often quoted the Lord's words, 'Come to Me all you who labour and are heavy laden and I will give you rest' and then appealed to them warmly. 'Who is there in this life who is not in labour in his sins? Christ said, "Come to Me all you who labour". Now, if He said that, why do you ascribe your failures to Him who invites you? Come! His house is not too narrow for you. Fly to God, who is present where you are standing. Cease this labour of yours and fly to His presence. The Son of God, by whom all things were made, calls to the human race, "Come to Me and learn from Me"' (*Sermon 38:18*). But, as old age began to close in upon him, he expressed himself to his international audience in such uncompromising fashion about God's irresistible will that he seemed to have obliterated what he believed about freedom of choice, overlooking biblical passages which invite all men to receive the good news, such as John 3:16. Perhaps it was the strain of prolonged controversy, along with the lack of humanising influence of wife and family, which became evident in the repetitiveness and unsympathetic severity of some of his later writings.

In his defence it must be admitted that he based his views on a large number of New Testament allusions to God's election of believers. This was not something he invented. Refusing to eliminate either God's sovereignty or human free will, he insisted 'We embrace both truths' (*City 5:9-10*). Yet his critics had substantial grounds for suggesting that he had distorted the gospel message, nullifying the attractive openness of Christ's words and Paul's preaching. He invited disagreement by reiterating in book after book that God had deliberately abandoned unbelievers to punishment as well as choosing believers for salvation, by denying that God desired everyone to embrace the truth, and by insisting that God's will invariably prevails. This appeared to turn the good news into bad news for most people, making God's incomprehensible will central to the Christian message rather than the inviting love of Jesus.

A similar alteration to biblical teaching is apparent in what he said about persevering in Christian faith. He was of course aware that many found it 'easy to hear about Christ and easy to applaud the preacher' but not so easy to endure through all life's struggles and temptations. 'There are many praising who will yet blaspheme, chaste who will yet be fornicators, sober who will hereafter wallow in drink, standing who by and by will fall' (*Tractate 45:12-13*). One day in Hippo he cried out to the people in his appealing way: 'You know very well that we are all fellow-disciples under one Master. I am not your master because I speak to you from this higher spot. He who dwells in us all is the Master of all. Just now He spoke to us in the reading from the Gospel and He said, "If you continue in My word then you are truly My disciples." I say the same to you. To be a disciple it is not enough just to come to Christ. He did not say, "If you hear My word", but "If you continue in My word". What is it to continue in His word but not to yield to temptation?' (*Sermon 84:1-2.*)

At the very end of his life he wrote a book beginning with

the words 'The perseverance by which we persevere in Christ even to the end is the gift of God', presenting it as a second aspect of predestination, which even he himself found mystifying. 'Those who are not to persevere, who fall away, are beyond all doubt not to be reckoned among the elect. And yet, seeing they believe and are baptized and live according to God, we in our ignorance call them elect. But God does not, for He knew that they would not have the perseverance which leads the elect forward into the blessed life. If I am asked why God should not have given them perseverance, I answer that I do not know. It is indeed greatly to be wondered at, that to some of His own children whom He has regenerated in Christ, to whom He has given faith and hope and love, God does not also give perseverance. Who would not be astonished at this?' (*Rebuke 18.*)

Such texts as I Corinthians 4:7, 'What do you have that you did not receive?' and James 1:17, 'Every good and perfect gift is from above', were constantly in his mind, yet it is regrettable that he did not give equal weight to the biblical exhortations to abide in Christ, resist the devil, deny yourself, stand fast, flee fornication, pursue righteousness, put on the armour of God, seek first His kingdom, fight the good fight, be filled with the Spirit, let the word of Christ dwell in you richly, and work out your own salvation. The New Testament never speaks of the gift of perseverance, but frequently demands disciplined obedience from all believers.

17

The City of God

Two of the more than ninety books Augustine wrote have attained particular fame. Best known is his *Confessions*. Second must stand *The City of God*, which is more difficult, lacks a connecting thread of narrative, and contains substantial passages of interest only to specialists. It is divided into twenty-two books, each of which has a number of short chapters. Many have been repelled by its size and the large number of topics treated in what appears to be a chaotic tome, but to the determined reader it offers rich rewards. Augustine wrote it in his maturer years, from 413 to 426, starting when he was fifty-nine and completing 'this huge work' when he was seventy-two.

Many of his other writings were composed to counter some doctrinal or practical threat to the faith, their Latin titles starting ominously with the word *Contra*, but *The City of God* was not written 'against' anybody, though it set out to challenge the contemporary inclination to blame Christianity for the fall of Rome. It constitutes a marvellous revelation of Augustine's alert mind ranging over the Bible and many aspects of life around him. Read carefully and repeatedly, with omissions to suit each reader's taste, it proves to be not a dark tunnel but a colourful pageant in which we meet hundreds of citizens of Roman Africa and get to know its most famous man as we can nowhere else. The *Confessions* shows us Augustine lost in life's maze, until found at last. 'You have made us for Yourself', he declared in its opening lines, 'and our hearts are restless till they rest in You.'

But in *The City of God* he had passed a long way down life's road, surveying not himself but the world around him, the Christian Church in the world, and the message of the Bible to Church and world alike. In the *Confessions* we meet the convert; in *The City of God* we meet the bishop at his maximum height of intellectual, prophetic and expository genius.

The title, *The City of God*, has dramatic biblical roots in the Epistle to the Hebrews and the Book of Revelation. It stands in contrast to Rome, the city of man, which had fallen at last. Throughout the book Augustine throws out memorable statements to show what he means by it. 'We, His City'; 'God's Church'; 'The redeemed household of servants of the Lord Christ'; 'Christians as they live by God's standards in the pilgrimage of this present life.' Apart from Rome, the counterpart to the City of God was another spiritual city, the devil's. 'I classify the human race into two branches: the one consists of those who live by human standards, the other of those who live according to God's will. I also call these two classes two cities, speaking allegorically. By two cities I mean two societies of human beings, one of which is predestined to reign with God for all eternity, the other doomed to undergo eternal punishment with the devil.' And he describes the City of God as itself consisting of two parts: the saints and angels already in heaven, and Christians still in this world. So he repeatedly refers to 'the pilgrim City of God', declaring that 'the heavenly city leads what we may call a life of captivity in this earthly city, as in a foreign land, and while on pilgrimage in this world she calls out citizens from all nations and so collects a society of aliens, speaking all languages.' This framework of ideas underlies the entire book. In expounding and illustrating it, apparently oblivious to time and length, Augustine's writing is rarely tedious and he so repeatedly captures our admiration by paragraphs of remarkable brilliance that, in spite of all its difficulties, *The City of God* retains its position among the great books of the world.

It also shows that the bishop of Hippo, toiling in his study, church and monastery, was by no means impervious to natural phenomena in the world around him. Amidst weightier matters it reveals his interest in very small creatures: in mice, newts, locusts, beetles, bees, flies, fleas, worms and frogs, for he frequently mentions them. He suggested that 'even the most savage beasts safeguard their own species by a kind of peace, cherishing and rearing their young, though most of them are not gregarious like sheep, starlings and bees, but solitary like lions, eagles and owls. What tigress does not gently purr over her cubs and subdue her fierceness to caress them? What kite however isolated as he hovers over his prey, does not find a mate, build a nest, help to hatch the eggs, rear the young birds and, as we may say, preserve with the mother of his family a domestic society as peaceful as he can make it?' And he was perplexed to know how wild animals came to be on the remoter Mediterranean islands, 'so far from the mainland that it is clearly impossible for any beasts to have swum to them'.

He was convinced that there were 'immense tracts of space outside the world' and that the place occupied by the earth was 'so tiny a space compared with that infinity'. He suggested that the better an observer's sight the more stars he sees 'and so we are justified in supposing that some stars are invisible even to the keenest eyes quite apart from those which, we are assured, rise and set in another part of the world far removed from us'. He thought Asia covered half the world, Europe and Africa the other half, and 'the reason why Europe and Africa are treated as two separate parts is that between them the water enters from the Ocean to form the intervening sea, our Great Sea'.

In *The City of God* Augustine expressed his regret that most people were ignorant of history, for his own studies had led him to the conclusion that 'only illiterates imagine there is something extraordinary in the mishaps of their own time and that they did not happen in other periods'. The horrors of the past and the shocking realities of the present were part of his daily thinking. 'I am sick of recalling the many acts of revolting injustice, all the torrents of bloodshed, all the greed and monstrous cruelty, the disgusting infection of crime and immorality which rages, and the lust for power which of all human vices was found in its most concentrated form in the Roman people as a whole.' He lamented the pursuit of perverted delights by the freedom-loving majority whose spokesmen maintained that 'anyone should be free to do as he likes' and argued for a plentiful supply of prostitutes, suggesting that 'anyone who disapproved of this kind of happiness should rank as a public enemy'. The cruelty of the courts, 'the wickedness of the wise man in his judicial capacity', deeply distressed him. He found it 'an unthinkable horror that innocent witnesses should be tortured in cases which are no concern of theirs, or that the accused are frequently overcome by the anguish of their pains and so make confessions and are punished despite their innocence, so that the judge still does not know whether it was a guilty or an innocent person he has executed'.

Surveying the social and moral conditions of the Empire, Augustine deduced that he was living in a world 'full of the allurements of impure pleasures, maddened with all its monstrous cruelties, menacing with all its errors and terrors'. When Rome's very triumphs had given way to 'wars of a worse kind, social and civil wars', he asked whether it was sensible to boast of the extent and grandeur of the Empire when 'you cannot show that men lived in happiness as they passed their lives under the shadow of fear and amid the terrors of ruthless ambition'. In addition to these public evils, he was constantly confronted with distressing personal situations, with men whose limbs never stopped shaking, others whose arms or legs had had to be amputated, some who were blind as well as deaf, one whose 'spine was so curved as to bring his hands to the ground, turning the man into a virtual quadruped', and many who had gone raving mad. 'Who is competent, however torrential the flow of his eloquence, to unfold all the miseries of this life?'

In spite of this catalogue of horrors, he did not agree with those who considered suicide justifiable to escape pain, torture or rape. To prevent rape by suicide was, in his opinion, merely adding one's own crime to the other person's. 'It is significant that in the sacred canonical books there can nowhere be found any injunction or permission to commit suicide, either to ensure immortality or to avoid evil. In fact we must understand it to be forbidden by the law "You shall not kill". To kill oneself is to kill a human being and those guilty of their own death are not received after death into a better life.'

It was also in *The City of God* that Augustine was able to divorce himself from the pressure of episcopal duties which normally dictated the course of his writing. Here he found time to contemplate 'the natural abilities of the human mind and the astounding achievements of human industry' in agriculture and navigation, in pottery and sculpture, in painting and poetry, in the capturing and taming of wild animals, in making weapons to destroy life and improving medical care to preserve it, in music, geometry, arithmetic and astronomy. 'It is God who has given man his mind', he declared. He saw unmistakable evidence of the same 'Almighty Artist' in the versatile human body with its 'complex system of veins, sinews and internal organs', its erect posture so different from that of 'irrational animals which generally have their faces turned towards the ground', and the marvellous mobility of tongue and hand, 'so adapted for speaking and writing and for the accomplishment of a multitude of arts and crafts'.

To these good gifts of God he added 'the diversity of beauty in sky and earth and sea; the abundance of light and its miraculous loveliness in sun, moon and stars'; the charm of fire, so useful 'with its heat, its comfort and its help in cooking'; the multitudinous varieties of birds with their songs and their bright plumage; the countless different species of living creatures of all shapes and sizes; the abundant supply of food; the welcome alternation of day and night; the soothing coolness of breezes; all the material for clothing provided by plants and animals: and 'the mighty spectacle of the sea, putting on its changing colours like different garments, now green with many varied shades, now purple, now blue'.

In the final two hundred pages of the book Augustine set out his view of things to come. He never taught anything about purgatory. Knowing that some people stressed it, he suggested 'it is not impossible' but treated it as doubtful, since it hinged on 'an obscure saying in I Corinthians 3 which must be interpreted so as not to conflict with plain statements of the apostles' (*Enchiridion 68-69*). And he had abandoned belief in a literal millennium and instead applied the term to the period 'from the first coming of Christ to the end of the world, which will be Christ's second coming'. Though he acknowledged that during this time the devil is allowed to test Christians, he was convinced that God had 'thrown him out from their inner man and tied him up among those who belong to his party'. From the concluding verses of the Old Testament he deduced that Elijah is to reappear and cause the Jews to turn to Christ. After that he anticipated a brief period of intense persecution under

Antichrist, followed by Christ's return. 'He will come, whether we like it or not. Let us not resist his first coming, that we may not tremble at his second coming.' Then the dead will rise and the good and the wicked will be separated. 'Here and now we are not separated from the unrighteous by the place where we live, but by character, by desires, by faith, hope and love. We live together, though our life is not the same. But in the end there will be an open separation, a distinguishing not just of character and wisdom but of life and bodies, to which the Apostle Paul appears to point with his finger when he says "This corruptible must put on incorruption" (I Cor. 15:53 in the original Greek text). Being with Christ is not so much interrupted as glorified by the resurrection. All the dead are sleeping, both good and bad. The good have joy, the evil torments. But when the resurrection takes place, the joy of the good will be fuller, the torments of the wicked heavier. Good believers have been received into peace, but all of them have still to receive the fulfilment of the divine promises, the resurrection of the flesh and eternal life. The rest given immediately after death to every one worthy of it is received as each one dies. So some have been in that rest a long time, others not long. But when they awake from this sleep, they will all together receive the promised resurrection of the flesh' (*Tractate 19:18, 49:10, Letter 55:14:25*).

Then follows the last judgment. He thought he was probably right in suggesting this order of events, though he admitted there were many obscure statements in the Book of Revelation, 'principally because our author repeats the same thing in many ways, so that he appears to be speaking of different matters though in fact he is treating of the same subject in different terms'.

Augustine was emphatic that the punishment of unrepentant

sinners will be eternal. He rejected the opinion of 'compassionate Christians' that God in His love would never allow such a thing. 'Our friends who long to get rid of eternal punishment should cease to argue against God and instead obey God's commands while there is still time.' It was obvious to him that 'the phrases "eternal punishment" and "eternal life" are parallel' and that it was unwise for people to suppose 'that what is to happen is not what the Scriptures speak of but what they themselves would like to happen'.

Then he surveyed the bliss in store for those who have been emancipated from the powers of darkness and transferred into the kingdom of Christ, 'liberated from this life of misery, a kind of hell on earth, through the grace of Christ our Saviour'. He looked forward to true peace under no attack from within or without, when God would be seen uninterruptedly, perfect freedom of the will would be experienced together with the inability to sin, and everything unlovely would be excluded.

18

Monks and Miracles

There were always talented men living in the monastic community over which Augustine presided in Hippo. He found biblical support for this way of life in the opening words of Psalm 133, 'How good and pleasant it is when brothers live together in unity.' In his commentary on the Psalms he explained that 'these words begat the monasteries'. He linked them to the statement in the Acts of the Apostles that at first 'the believers had everything in common' and 'no one claimed that any of his possessions was his own'. From his experiences in Milan, when 'You converted me to Yourself, so that I no longer sought a wife' (*Confessions 8:12*), he retained an optimistic impression of men who 'discarding the pleasures of this world, live together in a chaste and holy society, passing their time in prayers, readings and discussion, without pride, contention or envy. Their life is one of perfect harmony and devotion to God' (*Morals 31:67*).

In the course of time he had bad as well as good experience of such communities, but the perversity of a minority, their laziness and immorality, did not alter his conviction that this was the ideal way for Christians to live. 'As I have hardly found any men better than those who have done well in monasteries, so I have not found any men worse than monks who have fallen. If we are grieved by some foul blemishes, we are comforted by a much larger proportion of good examples' (*Letter 78:9*).

Diligent study of the word of God characterized the

monastery at Hippo. It served as a theological seminary, a training school for dedicated men, some of whom did not stay there permanently but went to pastor churches in other towns, where they established mini-monasteries on the same pattern.

Recalling Paul's advice in 2 Thessalonians 3:10, 'If a man will not work, he shall not eat', Augustine wanted monks to support themselves by manual labour, though others disagreed, quoting Christ's saying about birds God feeds, although they neither sow nor reap. He felt that men who expected to be supported by the gifts of working people were simply giving way to laziness. He was concerned to find that their admirers 'preached them up as holier men'. In his view responsible monasticism, which combined study and prayer with regular hours set apart for 'a common workman's lowly toil', was being brought into disrepute by 'so many hypocrites under the garb of monks, strolling about the provinces, sent nowhere, fixed nowhere, some hawking the limbs of martyrs – if indeed of martyrs –', and all of them asking for money. He did not hesitate to call such behaviour devilish. And he also denounced the habit some of them had of letting their hair grow long. 'I shrink from saying more against this fault out of respect for certain long-haired brethren in whom, except for this, I find much to admire.'

His sister was in charge of the convent nearby, which he rarely visited. Augustine himself had devised the rule under which the nuns lived. All property, including their clothes, was held in common. Girls from poor homes found themselves living in comparative luxury, while others had to learn a new discipline. Any presents brought by parents for their daughters were not kept for private use, but added to the common stock under control of the prioress. To conceal a gift received was treated as theft. There were regular times of prayer and of fasting. A bath was allowed only once a month. Meals were taken in silence, listening to a reader. Hair had to be completely covered. No one was allowed to look fixedly at any man, particularly in church. 'A wanton eye is the index of a wanton heart.' The prioress was to be obeyed as a mother charged with the special responsibility of seeing that the rules were observed. Negative though some of these regulations may seem, it has to be remembered that Augustine was providing an alternative way of life for girls often married off when they were barely teenagers.

Heavily involved as he was in counselling monks as well as nuns, he often felt embarrassed at not being one of them. 'As far as concerns my own convenience, I would much rather do some work with my hands at certain hours every day, as is the rule in well-run monasteries, and have the remaining hours free for reading and praying, than be compelled to endure the intensely annoying perplexities arising from other men's disagreements about secular matters, on which I have to adjudicate. I can scarcely breathe for the pressure of such duties imposed upon me by men compelling me to go with them one mile, with whom our Lord commands us to go further. I am unable to excuse myself from such matters, even though I would prefer to do what I exhort you to do, instead of what I am forced to do' (*The Work of Monks 37*).

In writing to a community of monks on an island off the north coast of Sardinia, he contrasted 'the undisturbed rest which you enjoy in Christ' with his own arduous labours, yet he advised them that 'If the Church calls you to active service, guard against declining it through laziness, but obey God, who will guide you. Do not prefer your own ease to the claims of the Church, for if no good men were prepared to minister to her the beginning of your own spiritual life would have been impossible' (*Letter 48:1-2*).

The Apostle From Africa

A friend of Augustine who had returned to Africa from Bethlehem brought with him some bits of bone and handfuls of dust alleged to be relics of the earliest Christian martyr, Stephen. Someone had had a vision as a result of which these scraps were unearthed at Gaza. An irrational veneration of martyrs and their supposed remains had become very popular in the century since state persecution of Christians had ceased, but for several years Augustine did not actively promote the cult. These bogus relics of Stephen, killed in Jerusalem almost four hundred years previously, were deposited in small shrines throughout Roman Africa. In 424 a chapel was built containing a few grains of venerated dust alongside the church at Hippo.

Augustine did not oppose the innovation. In fact he was increasingly impressed by the miracles of healing which were reported to have occurred in connection with the relics. In one of his sermons he declared that 'Stephen has visited our country after his death'. In an age when there was little relief for pain, stories of alleged cures had tremendous appeal. There was a natural tendency to welcome and exaggerate miraculous events which seemed to confirm faith. Feeling that 'signs of divine power like those of olden days were frequently occurring in modern times too', Augustine initiated public readings of such stories. He knew a bishop, waiting for an operation on a painful ulcer, who was instantly healed while carrying relics of Stephen in a procession. A blind woman was cured by pressing to her eyes a bunch of flowers carried by another bishop while he held the relics. A priest died, 'his thumbs already tied together', but when someone rushed his tunic to the martyr's shrine and then laid it on his body, he recovered. A child playing in the square was crushed by the wheel of a runaway ox cart and lay writhing at the point of death. 'His mother snatched him up and placed him in the shrine. He not only revived but showed no sign of injury.' One marvel begat another. Raisings from the dead followed thick and fast, thanks either to clothes taken to shrines and hurried back to the body, or to prayer as the corpse lay beside the relics, or to anointing with St. Stephen's oil. Each healing was instantaneous and perfect, growing more fantastic at every telling. Truth and fiction became inextricably intertwined.

A climax was reached with the coming of the Cappadocian tremblers. Seven brothers and their three sisters had been laid under such a curse by their widowed mother that they were all afflicted with a frightful trembling of the limbs. The sight proved so fascinating to their fellow citizens that they 'took to wandering wherever the whim suggested and in this way visited almost every part of the Roman world'. When two of these professional beggars, Paulus and his sister Palladia, visited Africa they created a great sensation. 'They arrived at Hippo about a fortnight before Easter and attended church every day, visiting the shrine of the glorious martyr Stephen' (*City 22:8*).

On Easter Sunday morning, when a huge congregation had assembled, Paulus was the centre of attraction, holding on to the grating of the shrine as he prayed. Suddenly he fell flat on his face and then stood up, healed. 'The whole church was filled in every corner with shouts of thanksgiving', Augustine recorded. 'They ran with the news to me where I was sitting, ready for the procession. They came rushing one after another, each telling me, as though it was fresh news, what I had been told by the one before.' Paulus too presented himself to the bishop, 'bent down at my knees, then straightened himself up to receive my kiss'. They went into the church, packed to the doors with an excited mass of people, shouting with joy and praising God. 'At last silence was restored and the appointed lessons from Holy Scripture were read.'

After Augustine had preached, 'the man had breakfast with us and gave a detailed account of the whole tragic history of himself, his brothers, his sisters, and his mother'. Augustine had an official record of the event drawn up and on the following Wednesday there was another great gathering. 'I made the brother and sister stand on the steps of the bishop's throne, just below the level from which I addressed the people, while the narrative was read. The whole congregation, men and women alike, fixed their gaze on the pair, the brother standing without any untoward movement, the sister trembling in every limb.' He then asked the couple to withdraw while their case was discussed, but this was soon interrupted by loud shouts from the shrine containing the relics. No sooner had Palladia touched the grating than 'she fell down as if asleep and got up cured'. Pandemonium broke out when they brought her back into the church.

'Christian miracles', declared Augustine, 'are the work of God with the cooperation of the martyrs.' Although he made no attempt to justify this assertion from the Bible, it became his conviction that because the martyrs of former times had suffered for speaking the truth 'they have the power to perform miracles'. So he encouraged a cult of relics which was destined to proliferate in succeeding centuries (*City 22:10*).

19

Augustine Lives For Ever

In southern Spain the Vandals, after their long march from eastern Europe, had acquired a young commander named Gaiseric, a greater leader of men than any general Rome could put in the field for the next fifty years. In May 429 he assembled his people on the beaches of Andalusia, eighty thousand of them. It was not far to Africa from there, eight miles at the nearest point, for the hills on either side of the Strait of Gibraltar stand in full view of one another. So they crossed over.

Hippo lay a thousand miles east of their bridgehead and the whole coast was a maze of mountains, cut from north to south by innumerable rivers flowing off the Atlas ranges, abounding in good defensive positions. But the countryside was seething with discontent and fear, for the great days of Roman military might had passed away. At unbelievable speed the invaders moved eastwards. Possidius, Augustine's colleague ever since those first three years at Tagaste, recorded their advance as refugees began to arrive in Hippo with their tales of woe. 'And now, the divine will permitting, there appeared in a short time great forces of the Vandal army with whom were associated Alans, Goths and people of other races, all armed with spears and exercised in war. They crossed the sea in ships from Spain and, pouring into Africa, spread over the land, penetrating even into our province and district. They perpetrated all the cruelties and atrocities imaginable: robbery, murder, torturings, burnings and innumerable other barbarities, so that the country became depopulated. They respected neither age nor sex, nor priest, nor ministers of God, nor church buildings. Marauding and destroying came these ferocious hordes.' He was not exaggerating. Even the English language retains the word 'vandal' to this day.

Some Christian ministers living in the path of the invasion asked Augustine's advice whether or not to evacuate. Though reluctant to forbid anyone to move to what appeared to be safer places, he reminded them that it was their duty to stand by the churches they were called to serve, and he quoted verses in the Psalms which speak of God as a defence and a strong tower. But a prominent bishop objected. Referring to Christ's words, 'When you are persecuted in one place, flee to another' (Matt. 10:23), he pointed out that Mary and Joseph got away into Egypt from Herod and that Paul escaped over the wall of Damascus in a basket. 'I do not see what good we can do to ourselves or to the people by continuing to remain in the churches', he wrote, 'except to see before our eyes men slain, women outraged, churches burned and ourselves expiring amid torments applied in order to extort from us what we do not possess.'

Augustine, who had had no personal experience of the horrors of war, was compelled to think again. He suggested that when a Christian leader became a marked man, as Paul was at Damascus, it was legitimate to leave, but when the whole community was in equal danger they should either evacuate together or the clergy should stay with the people. Alluding to Christ's words about the hireling who flees when he sees the wolf coming, he suggested that 'God is powerful to hear the prayers of His children and to avert those things which they fear', without realising that for the moment it was easier to say that in eastern Numidia. 'When dangers have reached their extremity,' he continued, 'and there is no possibility of escape by flight, an extraordinary crowd of persons of both sexes and all ages is wont to assemble in the church. If the ministers be at their posts through the strength which God bestows upon them, all are aided, some are baptized, others reconciled to the church. None are defrauded of the communion of the Lord's body; all are consoled, edified, and exhorted to ask God, who is able to do so, to avert all things which are feared, prepared for both alternatives.'

Turning seventy-six at this time, Augustine found he had reached the point at which one no longer wants to go anywhere. 'I might have come if it had not been winter', he wrote in declining an invitation, 'I might have braved the winter if I had been young.' He had plenty to do without moving from his desk. For several years he had had to cope with a much younger man named Julian, who had become the new spokesman of the views of Pelagius.

To Julian, Augustine was 'the Carthaginian', a kind of modern Hannibal threatening the Romans, the enemy of both marriage and free will, the distorter of the character of God, the advocate of fatalism. To Augustine, Julian was a perverter of Christian truth, an enemy of the grace of God and a poisoner of the minds of men, 'tearing in pieces the sheep redeemed at such a price'. Repeatedly condemned by Church councils, he paid a high price for his obstinacy and has been pilloried for heresy through succeeding ages. As usual with opponents of the bishop of Hippo, we know Julian's views mainly thanks to quotations Augustine made from his writings in order to refute them. The issues on which they differed were the doctrine of original sin and the precise relationship between God's grace and human free will, but these involved disagreement on such related matters as marriage, the sexual instinct, the fate of infants dying unbaptized and the efficacy of baptism.

Julian denounced Augustine for treating sexual desire, including the intercourse of married people, as an evil thing, thus denigrating the whole marriage relationship. 'Married people are not guilty', he insisted. 'The sexual impulse is ordained by God. Your assertion amounts to saying that original sin is actually derived from marriage.' He accused Augustine of denying any real free will to mankind and strongly protested against his view that God has predestined some to salvation, others to damnation. 'No one is forced by God's power either into evil or into good', he declared. 'Man does good or evil of his own free will, assisted by God's grace or incited by the suggestions of the devil.'

These formidable charges and countercharges proved to be merely the preliminary skirmishes of a prolonged verbal war. Point by point Augustine resisted him through hundreds of pages in his *Against Julian*. Over and over again he analysed the story of Adam and Eve. Over and over again he delved into the mysteries of marriage, the sexual instinct and the procreation of children. 'You are mistaken, my son', he announced in conclusion, 'wretchedly mistaken.' About nine years had passed since the start of their heated argument, but Julian was still tormented by Augustine's insistence that infants needed to be baptized if they were not to be justly condemned to an eternity in hell because of the infection of sin derived from Adam. 'Who was it', he demanded, 'who declared the innocent guilty, who was so heartless, so harsh, so oblivious of God and justice, who was so barbaric a tyrant, deserving the hatred of the human race, by failing to spare not only those who had not sinned but even those who were incapable of sinning? Who is this person who punishes the innocent? When you answer "God" you give us a real shock. The same God, you say, who commends His love towards us, who loved us and did not spare His own Son but gave Him up for us, He it is who passes this verdict, who persecutes newborn babies and assigns infants to eternal flames, infants whom He knows are incapable of either good or evil. What a cruel, blasphemous, pernicious belief! You have departed so far from piety, from culture, even from plain common sense, as to believe that your God is guilty of injustice.'

So in his old age Augustine, who in youth had dared to cross swords with Jerome, was himself confronted not only by the Vandals on the borders of Numidia but with an angry young man challenging his mature convictions and ridiculing him in public. He could not do much about the Vandals but he refused to let Julian go unanswered. Line for line, blow for blow, he retaliated, dictating far into the spring nights, refusing to modify his position in any way, for 'it was not I who devised original sin'. The Scriptures were open before him under the lamp: 'By one man's disobedience many were made sinners' (Rom. 5:19), 'Whoever believes and is baptized will be saved' (Mark 16:16), 'I tell you the truth, unless a man is born of water and the Spirit, he cannot enter the kingdom of God' (John 3:5), and many more which his fertile brain produced in abundance and marshalled with extraordinary skill. He was determined not to compromise, not to allow Julian to defeat him, not to exchange God's word for human sentiment.

Meanwhile he continued preaching to the troubled people of Hippo, his congregations swollen by refugees. 'Have you given all you had to the barbarians?' he asked them one day. 'I gave everything, but I stayed alive', was the reply, and he tried to make the most of it. 'You gave to the enemy so that you could go on living as a beggar. Give something to Christ so that you may live on in blessedness. You still have something. You have yourself. It is from the devil that you need to be redeemed, the devil who drags you with him to the second death, the eternal fire. To redeem yourself from the second death you need righteousness. Hold it fast, make it your own and you will be redeemed from the second death. Christ went through affliction, abuse, false accusations, spitting in the face, through a crown of thorns, through the cross.'

In the spring of 430 the Vandals surged forwards again through the mountains of Numidia. The only place they failed to take was Cirta, perched on its lofty crag. The Roman army withdrew to the coast at Hippo, while the Vandals went on to besiege Carthage. For the time being Hippo was safe, protected by its mountain, rivers, swamps and lofty ridges, with the sea-lanes open to Italy. Refugees poured in as the surrounding countryside was overrun. Happily, Possidius escaped in time to join Augustine, for he was the only man on either side to leave any account of what happened. On the plain outside Hippo and up in the hills, all the towns were burnt and the population decimated, 'given over to torture, slain by the sword, sold into captivity'. Others got away to hide in woods and rocky mountains, where death from starvation soon stared them in the face. In Hippo they had first-hand evidence of the magnitude of the disaster. Nothing was hidden from Augustine. 'Tears were his bread day and night', recorded Possidius. 'They were mournful and bitter beyond all others because of his old age and because life was now nearing its end. We remember that whilst sitting together and conversing at table Augustine said to us, "You must know that in this time of calamity I have prayed to God that He might deliver this city and, if this was not His holy will, that He would give strength to His servants to submit to His decrees, and also that He might be pleased to take me to Himself out of this world." And saying this whilst we listened, every one of us who were in the city with him prayed together to the good God.'

During the first three months of the siege of Hippo, Augustine went on with his usual work of preaching and writing. 'He was sound in all the members of his body and enjoyed good sight and hearing.' 'As you can see,' he said in one of his last sermons, 'in years I have only recently become an old man, but in physical weakness I have long been old. But I shall not desert you. Pray for me that I may serve you in the word of God as long as there is life in this body.'

In the great heat of August he was forced to take to his bed, exhausted by fever. He ceased dictating several books on which he was still working, for 'this was his last illness, nor did the Lord withhold from His servant what he sought in his prayers'. As he lay there, white-haired in the doomed city, an invalid came to be healed. 'If I possessed any such gift of healing,' said Augustine, 'don't you think I would use it in my own case first?' However, when the man explained that God had told him in a dream to go to the bishop, he relented and laid hands on him.

Then he asked his companions to write out the seven so-called Penitential Psalms – Psalms 6, 32, 38, 51, 102, 130 and 143 – and hang them up on the wall of his room so that he could see them as he lay in bed. 'He recited them continuously and whilst he did this he shed bitter and abundant tears.' He wanted to end his life in humility, remembering how great a sinner he had been. He did not weep because he was afraid to die, for 'with Christ death is not to be feared', nor had he any doubts about what lay beyond it. 'When the final judgment has been completed there will be two kingdoms, the one Christ's, the other the devil's, the one consisting of the good, the other of the bad. The former will live happily in eternal life. The reward of virtue will be God Himself: we shall see Him for ever, we shall love Him without satiety, we shall praise Him without weariness. After all God's works, He rested on the seventh day and the voice of His book tells us that after our works we also will rest with Him in the sabbath of everlasting life' (*Enchiridion III, City 22:30*).

Repentant and trusting in 'the Mediator, through whom we climb from the depths to the heights', he lay there for a few weeks, remembering. 'And lest his reflections might be disturbed by anyone during the ten days before he died, he asked to be left alone and that no one would enter his room except when the doctor came to see him or his food was being brought. We observed his wishes and did not disturb him. He spent all the time in prayer.' So at the last he did attain that total separation from earthly distractions which had beckoned him ever since the months at Cassiciacum. And then, on 28 August 430 'while we stood around him, watching him and joining him in prayer, he sank into sleep with his fathers. And for his eternal repose on the day of his burial the holy sacrifice was offered up, at which we were all present. He made no will, for as a poor man of God he had no possessions.' Soon afterwards Possidius, the first and most important of Augustine's many biographers, set down the main facts not already made public in the *Confessions* about 'that great man with whom I lived for nearly forty years in the closest friendship and in all sweetness, without trouble or disagreement'. He felt that those who had actually seen Augustine, listened to him and been intimate with him had benefited from his life beyond all others, although in his numerous books 'it can be seen how, with God's help, Augustine became so great in the Church and in these works the faithful shall find that Augustine lives for ever'.

The storm of the world went on. After the siege had lasted another eleven months, the Romans evacuated Hippo and the Vandals burnt it. Four years later Carthage fell to them and

Gaiseric became master of the central Mediterranean, even in his turn sacking Rome. For a hundred years the Vandals prevailed, dealing rigorously with the Catholic Church, whose buildings were confiscated and clergy expelled. But Roman power survived in Constantinople and when eventually North Africa was recaptured, the Vandals lost their racial identity and disappeared. The most decisive conquest of all took place around 650 when the Arabs poured in triumphantly, bringing with them their language and a new religion, Islam. Before long both Punic and Latin fell into disuse, though the original Berber languages continued to be spoken in the mountains. Arabic became dominant and has remained so to this day.

But it was not only Roman rule and the Latin tongue which deserted that splendid coast. Hippo itself was abandoned. In time earth covered the old town; crops were planted, goats grazed, and houses were built over it. For a thousand years it was a lost city. Not until 1924, during the period of French rule in Algeria, was it excavated and men gazed in amazement at the skeleton of Augustine's church and walked the massive paving stones he knew so well. Then the French left, as the Romans had left, and the site began to silt up once more. Trees, weeds and goats have returned, while the roads and factories of the sprawling town of Annaba threaten to engulf the silent city.

In the centuries that followed the coming of the Arabs, visible evidence that many people in North Africa had trusted in Jesus Christ became confined to the ruins of their church buildings and the books written by Augustine, thanks to which it is still true that the bishop is speaking. 'In this wicked world and in these evil times, the Church through her present humiliation is preparing for future exaltation. Trained by the stings of fear, the tortures of sorrow, the distress of hardship, and the dangers of temptation, she rejoices only in expectation. After sowing the seed of the gospel, Christ suffered, died, and rose again, showing by His suffering what we ought to undergo for the cause of truth and by His resurrection what we ought to hope for in eternity. In the sight of His disciples He ascended into heaven and sent them the Holy Spirit He had promised. Amid terrible persecution the gospel was then proclaimed throughout the entire world, the Church proceeding on its pilgrimage from that time up to the end of history' (*City 18:49-51*).

Maps and Diagrams

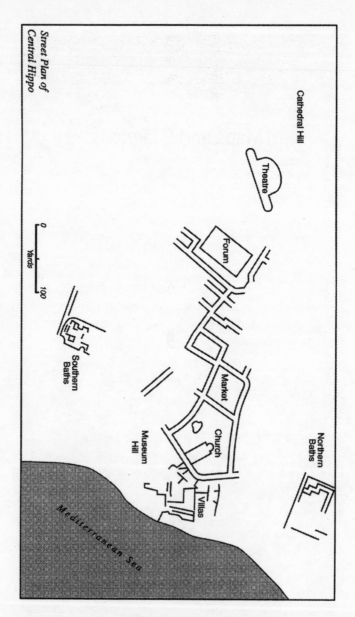

Fig. I Street Plan of Central Hippo in Augustine's time

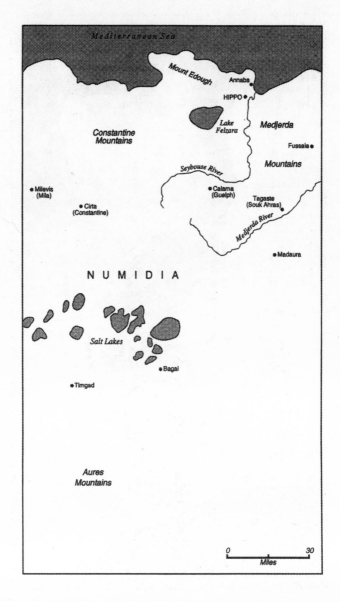

Fig. 2 Numidia in Augustine's time

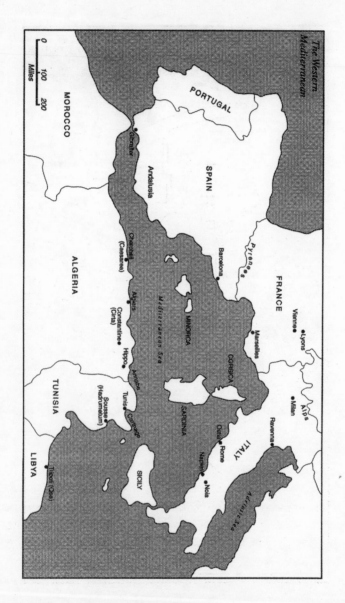

Fig. 3 Western Mediterranean

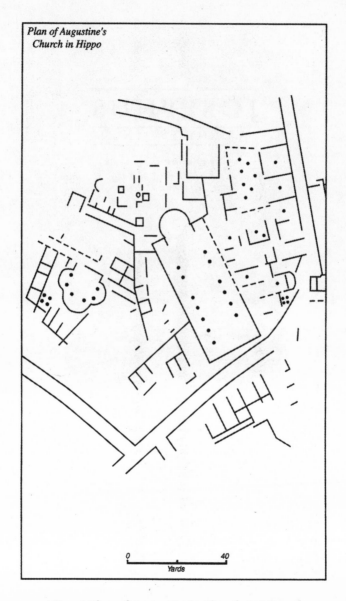

Plan of Augustine's Church in Hippo

0   40
Yards

Fig. 4 Plan of Augustine's Church in Hippo

Flavius

JOSEPHUS
A UNIQUE WITNESS

*Independent Evidence
confirming the
New Testament Story*

*This is a helpful introduction to an important
first century historian. It concentrates on
how his writings relate to the New Testament,
frequently confirming its history and
illuminating its context.*

Oliver Barclay,
Leicester

David Bentley-Taylor

Josephus, A Unique Witness

Independent Evidence confirming the New Testament Story
David Bentley-Taylor

Is there any extra-biblical data about the times in which Jesus lived?

Thanks to Josephus, the religious, social and political environment familiar to Jesus and the apostles springs to life in his pages. Here is a readable selection from his extensive writings, confirming the New Testament documents.

'Josephus was a first century Jew living in Jerusalem during most of the events recorded in the Acts of the Apostles... Josephus was not a Christian, but he knew about John the Baptist and Jesus... He was a man of action and a talented historian, describing in detail the terrible struggle between the Romans and the Jews in which he himself played so significant a role.'

'This is a helpful introduction to an important first century historian. It concentrates on how his writings relate to the New Testament, frequently confirming its history and illuminating its context.'
Dr Oliver Barclay

'David Bentley-Taylor has done an excellent job in reviewing the works of Josephus and particularly bringing to out attention the points at which Josephus's account touches on the background to the NT an incidents we find there.'
Evangelicals Now

ISBN 1 85792 499 1

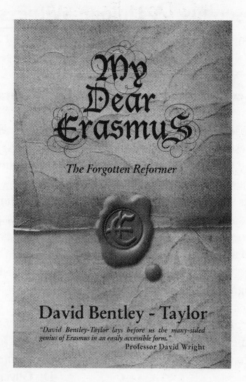

My Dear Erasmus

The Forgotten Reformer

David Bentley - Taylor

*"David Bentley-Taylor lays before us the many-sided
genius of Erasmus in an easily accessible form."*
Professor David Wright

My Dear Erasmus

The Forgotten Reformer

David Bentley-Taylor

Erasmus was born in 1469, so it might not seem surprising that he is little known today, but to many of his contemporaries he was the greatest man alive, a modern Socrates whose learning and wisdom had not been equalled for a thousand years, *'a kind of divine being sent down to us from heaven.'*

500 years after his birth, the University of Toronto Press began to publish the *'Collected Works of Erasmus'* in English in 86 large volumes. These include his massive correspondence with kings and popes, cardinals, bishops and theologians, professors and headmasters, philosophers, humanists and doctors, businessmen, bankers and lawyers. Anyone who was anyone at some stage penned the words 'My Dear Erasmus....'

His was the most daring research into the human condition, and its responsibilities, of his time.

The march of history has not been kind to Erasmus. In spite of his phenomenal achievements he has been forgotten - eclipsed by Luther and concealed behind the Reformation. Yet the influence of Erasmus contributed powerfully to the Reformation, and this book is a much needed look at a man who's impact on history has long been underestimated.

'He deserves to be better known - and to be more widely enjoyed. Contemporaries called this razor-sharp writer one of the wonders of the world. This attractive presentation of him is painted largely in his own words from his masterly letters. David Bentley-Taylor lays before us the many-sided genius of Erasmus in an easily accessible form."

Professor David Wright, New College, Edinburgh

ISBN 1 85792 6951

Christian Focus Publications
publishes books for all ages

Our mission statement -

STAYING FAITHFUL
In dependence upon God we seek to help make his infallible word, the Bible, relevant. Our aim is to ensure that the Lord Jesus Christ is presented as the only hope to obtain forgiveness of sin, live a useful life and look forward to heaven with him.

REACHING OUT
Christ's last command requires us to reach out to our world with his gospel. We seek to help fulfill that by publishing books that point people towards Jesus and for them to develop a Christ-like maturity. We aim to equip all levels of readers for life, work ministry and mission.

Books in our adult range are published in three imprints.

Christian Focus contains popular works including biographies, commentaries, basic doctrine, and Christian living. Our children's books are also published in this imprint.
Mentor focuses on books written at a level suitable for Bible College and seminary students, pastors, and other serious readers; the imprint includes commentaries, doctrinal studies, examination of current issues, and church history.
Christian Heritage contains classic writings from the past.

For a free catalogue of all our titles, please write to
Christian Focus Publications, Ltd
Geanies House, Fearn,
Ross-shire, IV20 ITW, Scotland, United Kingdom

For details of our titles visit us on our website
www.christianfocus.com